Praise For The Author

"Russell is a leader in the Emergency Management arena with a genius for being able to provide informative, useful educational training seminars and workshops to the highest levels of the organisation. His engaging, interactive approach ensures those involved with the process genuinely understand and appreciate all aspects of their role. He is a consummate professional with a commitment to sharing his expertise and knowledge and it's a pleasure to see that he has continued to share his experience and knowledge of decision making under adversity in this book."

- Caroline Kerr MBCI
Risk Management Coordinator at Women & Newborn Health Services (Western Australia Dept. of Health)

"If you've ever faced a difficult decision or been pressured to make a decision faster than you'd like, then this book is for you. Russell contrasts the paradox of making fast and effective decisions under adverse conditions, yet careful and considerate decisions using the same methodology. Businesses nowadays must remain agile to remain effective. Rapid but effective decision making at all levels of an organisation is a must and this book should be in your toolkit."

- Simon Levy
National Risk Manager

"I had the good fortune to serve with Russell in the South Australian Metropolitan Fire Service during the 1990s. Russell's keen acumen for effective command and control stood him in good stead. I'm pleased that he has chosen to use this experience and share his knowledge to benefit anyone who struggles with decision making whether that be in emergency situations, tight business deadlines or simply the everyday decisions that we all face. This book will assist the reader to understand that emergency decision making principles have far reaching benefits beyond Emergency Services.

- Greg Howard AFSM, MIFireE, JP
DipWHS BSocSc MEmergMgt
Commander at Metropolitan Fire Service South Australian

"Think - Decide - Act demystifies the realm of the emergency manager. Defending public safety relies on sound decision making principles. Russell's clear explanations and insight allows the reader to understand and use the very decision making techniques used by emergency services to 'move the ball forward' no matter what setting you find yourself in."

- David Jordan
National Operational Risk and Compliance Manager

"I've known Russell for almost fifty years and in that time I have appreciated his ability to cut to the chase without being confrontational. I am delighted that he has chosen to share his emergency service expertise and insights with us all and I believe that these 'tools of the trade' are equally as useful in everyday life as they are in emergency situations. If you've ever struggled with indecision, then here's the kick-start you need."

- Timothy Ireland
Senior Policy Officer
SA Road Transport Authority

THINK DECIDE ACT

Global Publishing Group

Australia • New Zealand • Singapore • America • London

How to Make Effective Decisions Fast Using Emergency Protocols

Russell Boon

DISCLAIMER

All the information, techniques, skills and concepts contained within this publication are of the nature of general comment only and are not in any way recommended as individual advice. The intent is to offer a variety of information to provide a wider range of choices now and in the future, recognising that we all have widely diverse circumstances and viewpoints. Should any reader choose to make use of the information contained herein, this is their decision, and the contributors (and their companies), authors and publishers do not assume any responsibilities whatsoever under any condition or circumstances. It is recommended that the reader obtain their own independent advice.

First Edition 2016

National Library of Australia
Cataloguing-in-Publication entry:

Creator: Boon, Russell, author.

Title: Think decide act : how to make effective decisions fast using
emergency protocols / Russell Boon.

ISBN: 9781925288148 (paperback)

Subjects: Decision making.
Thought and thinking.

Dewey Number: 153.83

Published by Global Publishing Group
PO Box 517 Mt Evelyn, Victoria 3796 Australia
Email Info@GlobalPublishingGroup.com.au

For further information about orders:
Phone: +61 3 9739 4686 or Fax +61 3 8648 6871

To those who run towards danger when others choose to flee.

This book is dedicated to all Emergency Service workers world-wide, professionals and volunteers. Those who are there when we need them most. Those who have the courage to go where others fear to and above all, those that have given the ultimate sacrifice in their service to others.

Thank you

Russell Boon

Acknowledgements

My thanks and gratitude to all those people who inspired, helped and contributed to this book.

To David Cassidines and Leigh Caulfield who both encouraged me to forge ahead and create my emergency management consultancy. Without your advice and reassurance I'd still be stuck in a corporate role.

To David Jordan and John Shepheard who have both been my greatly valued and appreciated emergency confidants and sounding boards for the emergency management industry generally.

Acknowledgement to my mum and dad, both of whom had to suffer through my childhood yet managed to keep me on the straight and narrow. Who supported me though a few career changes including my application, entry and basic training for the South Australian Metropolitan Fire Service. Thank you, I know it was a challenge but as parents, you wouldn't have wanted it any other way!

A special thank you to the firefighters of B Shift at station 43 Christies Downs, South Australia, with whom I served for most of my eighteen year career with SAMFS. You were dependable when an emergency struck and your friendship during the many hours in between was always appreciated.

To Tim Ferriss, Tony Robbins, Lewis Howes, Dr. Gary Klein and Red Adair. You all have talents that have inspired me to tackle emergency management and business in different ways. You all challenge me to think differently, to solve differently and communicate in ways that make a difference.

To all those too many to name who have served or are serving as emergency wardens in their workplace and who have made conducting emergency training and exercises such a rewarding experience. I thank you for the time and effort that goes largely unrewarded and unacknowledged by volunteering to step up when an emergency happens.

A big thank you to my publisher, Global Publishing Group and the fantastic team, Darren Stephens, Jackie Tallentyre, Kelly Mayne and Helen Busse, who's expertise has made this book a reality.

Lastly and most importantly, a special thank you for the support, love, understanding, friendship, encouragement and laughter of my wife Amanda. Without you I wouldn't be where I am today.

Contents

BONUS OFFER
FREE BONUS GIFT

To help you even further I've included a bonus set of interviews with other decision makers. During this interview series I delve into what and how other key players in a range of industries approach and make decisions.

In this series you'll hear tips and insights from leading and influential thinkers and decision makers including....

- Canadian and international crisis management guru
- Former Director of Emergency Management for The White House
- National Risk Manager for retirement living and aged care
- Australia's leading gender diversity expert
- And many more....

Feel free to check back occasionally for additional bonus resources as they become available.

Claim your free bonus gift by going to

www.RussellBoon.com/bonuses

Preface

Writing this book has been a challenge. I've struggled with all the afflictions of procrastination that many, many writers before me have succumbed to. Strange I know, when the underlying theme of this book is to make a decision and take action. I've been lured by the calling of the full dishwasher, the dirty carpet that needs vacuuming and finally rearranging my closet because my clothes weren't hanging in order of height or colour and most importantly ensuring all my socks were paired. Not quite obsessive-compulsive disorder but petty mindless activities all elevated to the status of important and urgent in preference to facing the dreaded 'blank page.'

There's nothing that galvanises action more than an immediate crisis. From prehistoric times when a sabre toothed tiger prowled into a Neanderthal's cave, through to the modern-age reporter having to file a news story before a deadline, it's the immediacy of a critical timeframe that really garners a decision and action.

It's easy to delay a decision, especially if there's no immediate consequence. There's a wealth of books, blogs and YouTube videos devoted to defeating procrastination and streamlining your workday. Perhaps the best example is the book Getting Things Done by David Allen. This has been a best seller for many years and yet it is simply a book of how to organise yourself. Mind-blowing tricks such as labelling folders so you can find them. Read email and either act on them, delete them or put them into the read-later folder. Focus on what you're doing and do it. Don't get me wrong, it's a good book and one that needed writing and one that has given permission to millions of readers worldwide to decide and act on their daily work chores. In a sense and on a small personal scale, the methods within describe a manner of setting your own timeframes or deadlines to decide and act on tasks each day.

However, wouldn't it streamline your business if you knew how police officers or military commanders make decisions, some even life risking, in the blink of an eye? If you or your team are wrestling with 'analysis paralysis' and projects seem to stagnate due to 'more data required' or a project leader 'just can't make up their mind' then read on. Not everyone has to make decisions with critical outcomes, made under tight timeframes, in ambiguous and uncertain circumstances like those in emergency services and medical, military and law enforcement agencies. The 'art' of emergency decision making can be learned and practiced. Hopefully, your business life or your everyday life in general, doesn't demand or require a daily routine of emergencies.

The mind of an emergency manager however, is a curious thing. Irrespective of whether they are 'in the mood' or not they must respond and take action. It doesn't matter if that's a paramedic, a firefighter or even a parent responding to a child's accident; it's that confluence of situation, decision, action, assessment and adjustment that transpires because of a critical situation. You've probably heard it recounted at office gatherings or amongst friends when someone recounts a story about an accident or situation they encountered. Oftentimes you'll hear, "We/I didn't know what to do." This book isn't about how to handle different types of emergencies. It will prepare you with the mind-set to approach these circumstances with more clarity, which will increase your chances of success.

As famous French scientist Louis Pasteur said, *"Chance favours the prepared mind."*

Introduction

"It's not knowing what to do, it's doing what you know."

- Anthony Robbins

Late one night, whilst on nightshift, my station responded to a reported house fire. The report of a house fire causes emergency dispatch to automatically respond with two fire appliances. My station housed two fire appliances so both engines departed from the station together. About half way into our journey to the scene of this fire, our accompanying fire appliance was rerouted to another reported house fire. Something that emergency service workers the world over will probably agree upon, is that you can go days or even weeks without responding to an emergency and the very moment you receive one call for help you get two. Nonetheless, upon arrival at the affected property we encountered plenty of smoke and onlookers standing in the street. We radioed in our arrival and reported confirmation that the property was substantially involved. At first glance it appeared that the fire originated from an upstairs room. The house was a semi-detached townhouse of two storeys.

As we got out of the fire appliance the neighbours and onlookers flooded us with information regarding how many occupants the house normally contained but more importantly, depending upon who we chose to listen to, there was a man, woman and two children thought to be still inside. In the flurry by well-meaning bystanders, the exact number of occupants varied. It was thought that the husband might be on shift work and therefore not home right now.

On this particular night shift I was the fire appliance driver and consequently pump operator. As such, I set about putting the pump into gear and assisting with rolling out a high pressure hose line that the two firefighters would use to combat the fire. It would also protect them whilst gaining access to the affected rooms and conducting a search for the children and mother thought to be inside.

The station officer began assessing the situation by observing the exterior of the building and questioning bystanders. He began relaying information to me via a two-way radio and also directing the two firefighters into the most accessible entrance to the property. Being a single appliance and crew responding to what is normally a double appliance scenario meant double the work for everyone until such time as backup arrived.

Both firefighters donned their breathing apparatus sets. They then took the high pressure hose line and began unreeling it as they advanced towards the property and eventually into the building. Because it was dark and vision was also obscured by smoke, the full picture of the situation was unclear to me. Besides, I had my end of the bargain to keep up and that was the continuous supply of water at the appropriate pressure to the hose line. The guys on the end of that line were depending upon it.

The Scania fire appliances we were using carried one thousand five hundred litres of water on board and generally that provided around nine minutes of water to one high pressure hose line (HP line) which is generally ample time to locate and source a water supply from the street mains or hydrants.

Before I could set about exploring the darkened street for the closest water source I received a call from the Fire Service Communications

Centre (ComCen) requesting a status update so that they could prioritise resources due to apparently three simultaneous emergencies. The radio report duly issued to the satisfaction of ComCen, I grabbed the necessary equipment off the appliance and headed down the street to search for a water source - all this in around four minutes.

Fortunately some thirty five metres away I encountered a street plug, which is essentially a manhole in the road containing a water outlet specifically designed to match the accompanying standpipe that fire services worldwide carry for just this occasion. To operate the street plug one must remove the manhole cover using a street key, which is simply a device with some lugs that fit into a corresponding hole that is then twisted and allows the cover to be extracted. Unless it's an emergency, in which case the cover will always be stuck firmly in place by years of cars driving over it and packing down dirt and other debris into the cracks around the cover which then forms like cement, pretty much guaranteeing that a cover will never be extracted with ease. Nonetheless, an additional device carried by the South Australian Metropolitan Fire Service uses a cam system to apply additional leverage to the cover and thus extracting it, should it not be removable by the hand held street key. Luckily, I chose to grab this device as well as a standpipe and also a turncock key when I first headed off in search of water. In the darkened street with my appliance radio now audible over the loud speaker embedded into the pump panel, I could hear that ComCen was again trying to make contact to relay an estimated time of arrival for our backup. For now they'd have to wait. I was at about the two minute mark with seven minutes or thereabouts of water supply left.

Extracting the cover from the hydrant street plug I shone my torch into the resulting dark hole to check the condition and angle of the street plug (hydrant). Whilst all firefighters can insert a standpipe and effectively fit it correctly, a quick look into the seldom used manhole often saves some time if you can see the angle of the plug or, like on this occasion, if it's full of dirt or mud. I quickly reached into the hole and scooped out a handful of earth. Fortunately it wasn't rock hard and I began clearing the dirt around where I would insert the turncock key. Three more handfuls of dirt made room for me to be able to insert my turncock key onto the turncock and with some effort begin to open the turncock by heaving on the crossbar of the key. An eruption of mud spewed from the manhole and as more water flowed the mud slowly turned to muddy water and finally to clearer water. This trick quickly clears most street plugs of excess dirt without spending valuable time hand digging out mud and dirt. Now I could insert, align and mount my standpipe from which I could connect a sixty-four millimetre hose and supply water to my appliance. Four minutes down and about five minutes of water supply left.

As I mounted the standpipe and flushed the hydrant some more, I could hear ComCen calling me again via the radio. I had to return to the appliance anyway to grab the sixty-four millimetre hose I required to connect my appliance to the standpipe I had just mounted (or in technical terms, 'shipped'). I ran back towards the appliance and whilst doing so, I started to prioritise my actions. Does ComCen really need additional information right now and will it help me (or us) if we know how far away back-up is? Should I grab a roll of sixty-four millimetre hose first, answer the radio, check via two-way radio with the station officer as to how things are going and/or check my pump panel to ensure all is as it should be at this point in time? Answer: Yes, I should. All of the above.

I ran back towards the appliance. Suddenly a woman loomed out of the darkness, clearly distraught. As I approached her I urged her to stand back as I had enough on my plate without providing comfort or running commentary to upset bystanders. Whilst running I was also communicating via my two-way walkie talkie with the station officer trying to gauge how things were going and if more (or less) pressure was required on the hose line and if any additional equipment was required or information sent to ComCen.

I slowed in passing to look at my pump panel and assess the all-important water level in my appliance's tank. As I did, the woman grabbed my arm and began crying that her husband was in the house. After making good their escape, he went back into the building to retrieve the children still inside. "You've got to find him," she pleaded.

Five minutes down and four minutes of water supply left. With so many tasks competing for my attention, things were hectic to say the least. Whilst questioning the woman as to where the children's bedrooms were and where and when she last saw her husband, I edged around to the rear of the appliance. This was where the rolls of sixty-four millimetre hose were stored that I required to connect my appliance to the standpipe that I had just shipped. I opened the appliance locker that contained the hose while I radioed the station officer. I had just collected a roll of hose out of the locker when the station officer replied. In between rolling out the hose and running back to the standpipe I relayed the information that I had just learned to him and recommended that he return to the appliance to consult further with the woman. Six and a half minutes down and two and a half minutes of water remaining. All things considered, it was looking like another busy but successful night as pump operator.

I connected the hose to the standpipe and began running back to the appliance with the opposite end of the hose. Unfortunately, Murphy's Law meant that I was about five metres short of hose which meant rolling out an additional length. No problem; it happens. I grabbed another roll of hose from the rear locker of the appliance and bowled it out along the road, allowing it to unroll leaving me holding both ends of the hose. I dropped the male coupling and took the female to the point at which the other hose line had exhausted its length and coupled the hoses together. I returned to the pump panel with the male hose coupling in hand ready to make the final connection to the appliance.

Six minutes down and three minutes of water supply remaining. Hose connected, the final step was just two more thirty five metre runs. One to turn on the water and one to return to the fire appliance and open the inlet valve and begin replenishing my water reserves. Because the flow from the standpipe would be greater than the output from one single high pressure hose line I would be in the comfortable position of supplying all the water required for fire-fighting whilst simultaneously refilling the appliance tank. A pump operator's optimum situation.

I began my final thirty five metre sprint listening to the relay of information via walkie talkie between station officer and the two firefighters inside the building. The station officer was confirming that the electricity supply to the property had been switched off. This is a huge safety precaution for firefighters who are about to start squirting water in large volumes into a building. More information regarding the location of the children's bedrooms was also being relayed at the moment I began to turn the water on and began watching my flat hose start to form a more traditional hose shape as water began its run through it to my appliance. I began running back to the appliance ready to open the pump's inlet valve upon the arrival of the water. Seven minutes down with just two minutes supply left - easy peasy.

Rounding the side of the appliance I shirt-fronted a man about fifteen kilos heavier than me but about the same height. We bounced backward off each other clearly both surprised by our encounter. The man however, was covered in black soot and had his eyes and nose streaming with tears and snot. He clutched his chest and exclaimed, “I can’t breathe!” collapsing backward onto one knee as he said it, then toppling sideways onto the roadway, unconscious.

I radioed immediately on my walkie talkie for assistance required at the appliance and began assessing the man’s condition. Unfortunately there was no reply on the radio but fortunately there was a pulse on the victim. However, no respiration. “Just great,” I thought to myself as I rolled the victim onto his side to check his mouth or airway for obstruction. I looked longingly at the tank’s inlet valve just metres away from me now and observed that my inlet hose was beginning to pressurise meaning that the water had charged the hose and was now ready and available. But I had a more pressing problem for the minute. The victim’s airway was clear and I rolled him onto his back. I wiped the mucus away from his mouth whilst depressing my walkie talkie button again and tried to establish contact, this time with anyone who was listening. “Man down! Urgent assistance required at the appliance,” I garbled out as I tilted the victims head backwards in preparation for expired air resuscitation. No reply.

I began the first of five quick breaths as the commencement of the mouth-to-mouth resuscitation process whilst hearing ComCen yet again via the radio loudspeaker on the pump panel requesting a situation report (sitrep) from the scene. Eight minutes down and it’s now anyone’s guess as to how long the last minute of water supply will actually last.

I looked up after five quick breaths and whilst listening for the resumption of breathing in the victim I wiped my mouth and spat some sooty saliva off into the darkness. I took one big breath which gave me enough wind to try my walkie talkie one more time. There may have been a reply but my breathing and my pulse were so loud in my own ears I would have missed it anyway. No response from the victim, I gave one more breath and quickly stood to make a dash for my inlet lever. I was guessing that I was in the final thirty seconds of water supply.

A scream rang out right behind me that scared the daylights out of me. The victim's wife, whom I had encountered earlier, had returned to the appliance and was now greeted with the sight of her unconscious husband lying in the road. Other voices quickly joined the cacophony and it took me only a few seconds to identify the voices as children. The crying began immediately and they surrounded the victim and me, crying and pleading with me to do something. I returned to my knees and gave the victim another breath and then sprung to my feet and made a dash for the appliance. I hit the inlet valve lever releasing the pressure in the hose and noting the seemingly grateful tone of the appliance pump change note and then turned on my heels to return to the victim. Descending to my knees yet again, I administered one more breath to the victim who convulsed and moved his arms. I radioed the same 'assistance required' message over the airwaves through my walkie talkie one more time, finally getting a response. About a minute later, the station officer returned to the appliance to survey the scene and used the appliance radio to call for an ambulance whilst I maintained care of the victim, tried to comfort the family and kept a watchful eye on the pump panel.

It was just another day (or night) at work.

Chapter 1

THE ANXIETY OF INDECISION

"People will choose unhappiness over uncertainty."

-Tim Ferriss

Chapter 1 – THE ANXIETY OF INDECISION

Let's face it, if we could predict or even schedule emergencies, wouldn't life be a breeze? Same too for other pressing issues, concepts, ideas, business start-ups, product launches, career change, holiday destination, buying a new home or car, moving to another city or country, getting married, getting divorced or starting a family. There's the quick and the dead.

This book is not necessarily about how to make snap or reckless decisions or about turning you into an all-conquering emergency management guru ready for every unforeseen challenge life throws at you or making you ready to punch fear in the throat and lead the huddled masses to utopia. It's about breaking down the barriers each of us may have to deciding and empowering ourselves to think clearly, decide in good time and act appropriately. Removing our inhibitions to making a decision, frees us to arrive at a decision more quickly and have more confidence to action that very thing we've decided upon.

A report released in January, 2016 called, "The Future of Jobs," by the World Economic Forum forecasts, on average, over one third of the skill sets of most occupations will require skills that are not yet considered vital for the role in today's marketplace.

The report surveyed over three hundred and fifty employers in nine different industries across fifteen of the world's leading economies. The results of which were used to predict how technological advancements would challenge labour markets to evolve and how employers and employees will need to evolve to adapt to the workplace of 2020 and beyond.

Consequently, the report reveals that in the 2020 marketplace the ability to observe, interpret, analyse, problem-solve and apply judgement and decision making as the most desirable skill sets for thirty six percent of all jobs across all industries. The ability to face and deal with novel (unique or never encountered before) problems is a skill set that is valuable currently and looks to be in high demand for the foreseeable future.

Briefly though, before we delve on into the ins and outs of decision making, it's important to clarify what problem solving and decision making means and how they interrelate with one another. Problem solving is a range of activities designed to analyze a situation systematically and generate, implement and evaluate solutions. Decision making is a mechanism for making choices at each step of the problem solving process. Decision making is part of problem solving and it occurs at every step of the problem solving process. They are not the same but have a symbiotic relationship in that effective problem solving will generate more than one option and then a decision must be made on which solution to implement.

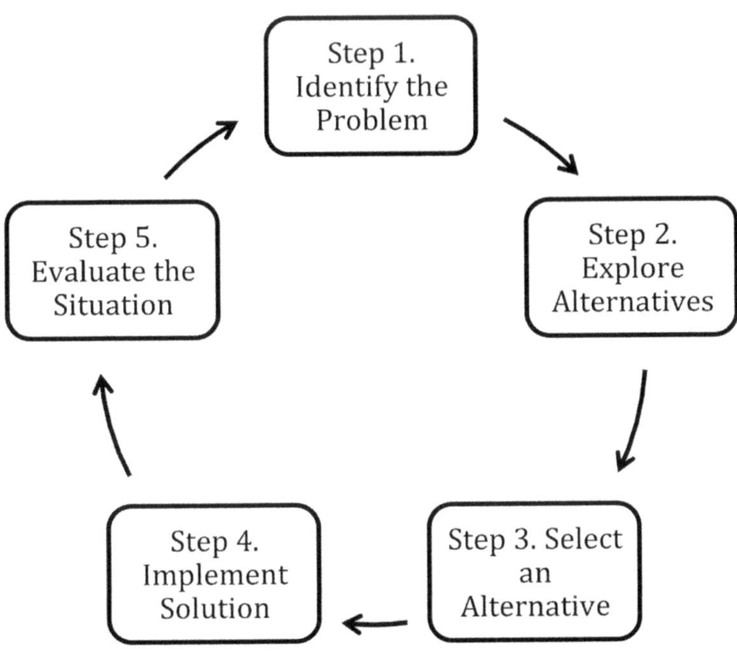

People once thought great chess players were great thinkers but they're not any better at general problem solving than the rest of us. They're just great chess players. Each and every one of us will bring their own unique life skills and knowledge to bear upon the choices and decisions we face. To decide upon a course of action to solve a problem, does not necessarily mean that each of us must develop an Einstein type intellect. We simply need to absorb as much information as possible regarding a range of options or choices, evaluate each one, then choose and try it. If it doesn't work, we now have more data upon which to re-evaluate our range of options.

Fire officers, military leaders, police, paramedics and doctors can all make life and death decisions almost instantly and yet the very same people may take ages to decide what can of beans to buy at the supermarket. Why and how can such critical decisions be made so fast, yet other much simpler decisions take some contemplation? Throughout this book we'll look at the ability of emergency management specialists to arrive at calculated decisions, in adverse and ambiguous conditions, with tight timeframes that are high risk and perhaps with limited resources and how you can apply those very same skills whenever you want to.

However, we've all been there; stuck in the moment. A decision should be made, in fact has to be made, yet it still does not come easily. There are many descriptions and metaphors for this paralysis that we all suffer from at various times. Perhaps you've used some of these yourself. "I was frozen like a deer in the headlights." "I was rooted to the spot" or "I was between a rock and a hard place."

Our mind has a tendency to magnify and distort unresolved decisions (making them appear more important or difficult than they might actually be) causing us stress and an inability to look at the decision rationally. Uncertainty breeds anxiety and anxiety undermines confidence and confidence underpins leadership. It can be a downward spiral during emergencies, in business or life in general. Take heed though, it can also be an upward spiral. Throughout this book we'll look at how you can build confidence in yourself and how that underpins decisiveness. Decisive and confident people are less prone to anxiety, a debilitating condition that affects over forty million adults in the United States alone.

Negative reactions to the choices, decisions and even dilemmas we confront daily are not always the result of our conscious thought. Our biology has a hand in how we react. Scientists have identified specific neural circuitry that can cause anxiety in some of us when we're faced with critical decisions. Our brains can actually judge how critical a decision is and produce anxiety in us accordingly.

One emerging field of research is neuroeconomics. It's essentially the blending of economics, psychology and neuroscience.

Neuroeconomic studies researching how humans make decisions, has suggested that anxiety and decision making share neural networks that overlap areas of the brain such as the striatum, the ventromedial prefrontal cortex, the dorsolateral prefrontal cortex and the amygdala. This overlap indicates that negative emotions like fear and anxiety determine how we calculate value before making a choice.

People suffering from severe anxiety tend to avoid situations that they perceive to be threatening and make decisions accordingly. Such behavioural traits and coping mechanisms can negatively impact on the quality of their lives.

Neuroeconomic research to establish how certain decision making situations can trigger anxiety in people, hopes to provide insight to counselors, psychologists and psychiatrists as well as pharmaceutical manufacturers when developing drug therapies.

UNCERTAIN? I CAN'T DECIDE

Author and productivity guru David Allen, in his book, 'Getting Things Done' talks about our capacity for memory and thought. He points us to an idea that scientists call 'distributed cognition,' meaning that at any given moment, we all have a number of unfinished ideas, tasks and commitments that roam around our brains wreaking havoc and occupying our finite "psychic RAM." Rumination over these ideas, tasks and commitments may result in distraction, worry or anxiety in more extreme cases.

Highly anxious people have more trouble deciding how best to handle life's uncertainties and may even 'catastrophise' seemingly normal or even trivial situations, interpreting them as much more than they really are. For example, they may have a disagreement with a spouse or partner and 'catastrophise' that into a doomed relationship or perhaps interpret a workplace change as a career threat. At the lesser end of the scale, thoughts about what potential outcome may result occupies our 'psychic RAM' and leads us into devoting energy to things that may never eventuate.

Anxiety and its sidekick, *worry,* feed on uncertainty. If a situation or a decision is not clear or the outcomes not immediately obvious, even unknown, then we humans react to this unpredictability. Of course, we'll all react differently depending upon our personality and the circumstances and magnitude of the decision we're facing. But one thing's for certain, humans love certainty.

Information is collected, analysed and decided upon by all of us, all the time, every day of the year, for all our lives. Why is it that some decisions are harder to make than others?

In 2015, scientists at the University of California, Berkeley, and the University of Oxford used decision making tasks, behavioural and physiological tests to assess people's response to unpredictability and its effect upon their ability to make logical and timely decisions.

The tests took thirty-one young and middle-aged adults whose baseline anxiety levels ranged from low to extreme. Each participant was tested by playing a computer based game involving both logical and probable outcomes. Probabilistic decision making requires using logic and probability to handle uncertain situations, drawing conclusions from past events to determine the best choice. Whilst the participant learnt the rules of the computer game, the circumstances of the game remained constant and thus logical and predictable. However, during another part of the game, the rules changed regularly and were thus less predictable. The participants who had reported their anxiety levels as high prior to the start of the test had more trouble than their less anxious counterparts when adjusting to the changes. An important skill in everyday decision making is the ability to judge whether an unexpected bad outcome is a chance event or something likely to recur if the action (decision) is repeated.

The researchers' results published in the journal, Nature Neuroscience, showed that anxiety may be linked to difficulty in using information about whether everyday situations are predictable or not and deciding how to react. In short, people prone to high anxiety have a tougher time reading the environmental cues that could help them avoid a bad outcome.

Another study by Marieke Jepma, PhD & Marina López-Solà in 2014, entitled Anxiety and Framing Effects on Decision Making: Insights from Neuroimaging, published in the journal of Neuroscience highlights how the "framing effect" plays a significant role during decision making activities and how it triggers anxiety.

How the outcomes are 'framed,' either positively or negatively, can significantly influence people's decisions in stressful situations. Meaning that people tend to make decisions based on the outcomes and whether they perceive them as gains or losses. The normal human reaction is to choose positively-framed options and avoid the negative ones. We'll look at framing specifically in the coming chapters and see how we can avoid some of its pitfalls and possibly use it to our advantage.

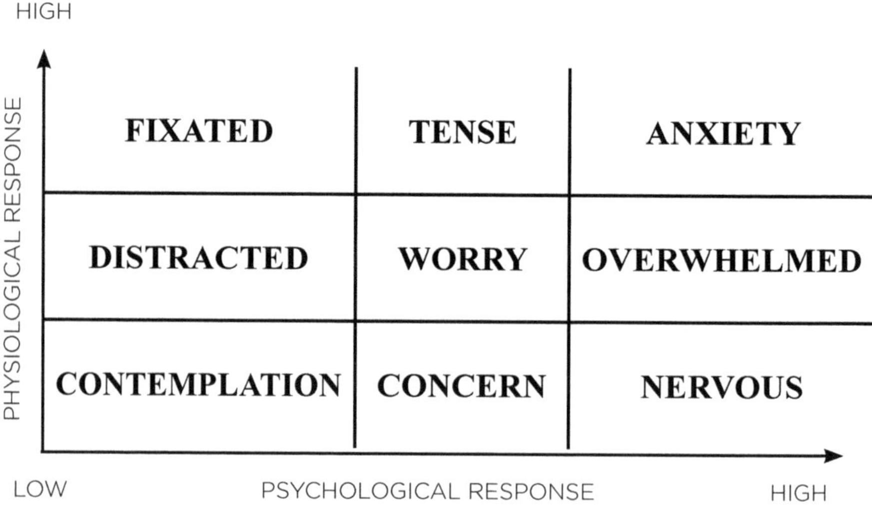

So as you can see, decision making can be the cause of a range of issues and yet mastering the art of timely and informed decisions can also be the cure. This is a chicken and egg scenario. The research cited above indicated that anxiety affects decision making ability and yet the ability to make good decisions in a timely fashion reduces uncertainty and thus anxiety. No matter where you see yourself in this cycle, having an enhanced ability to think, decide and act will build your resilience, equipping you to easily deal with life's challenges.

Delayed decisions can cause worry and anxiety by consuming our 'physic ram' or as it is more commonly referred to, 'playing on my mind.' The longer a decision is delayed without good cause the more out of proportion the difficulty of the decision can appear. There's never a right time. The right time is now.

As American humourist Erma Bombeck once said, *"Worry is like a rocking chair; it gives you something to do but never gets you anywhere."*

THE UPWARD SPIRAL

Napoleon Hill, author of the 1937 classic book, "Think and Grow Rich," studied over five hundred millionaires including well known investment and industry leaders such as Andrew Carnegie, Henry Ford and Charles Schwab.

Hill's analysis attributed success to one common trait. He wrote, "Analysis of several hundred people who had accumulated fortunes well beyond the million dollar mark disclosed the fact that *every one of them* had the habit of reaching decisions promptly."

This still appears to be the case almost eighty years later. Author Thomas C. Corley studied the daily habits of one hundred and seventy seven self-made millionaires over a five-year period, concluding that they avoid procrastination. Corely, like Hill, has studied what sets successful and wealthy individuals apart from others. In 2010, Corley released a book that set out his findings for wealth creation based upon his wealthiest clients, "Rich Habits – The Daily Success Habits of Wealthy Individuals" and more recently in another book "Change Your Habits, Change Your Life." Corely labels procrastination as a habit that must be banished writing that, "It prevents even the most talented individuals from realising success in life"

So the research indicates that these two human habits are a dichotomy that simply *must* be mastered for success to flourish. Hill considered that conquering procrastination (the opposite of decisiveness) was such an important role in accumulating wealth that he placed it as the seventh step of his thirteen steps toward becoming rich.

BEAT PROCRASTINATION? - I'LL DO IT TOMORROW

As humans, we have a tendency to prioritise what's important to us right now and not something that will affect us in the future, even if that future benefit is good for us. We seek immediate gratification in the present, especially if the payoff doesn't become apparent until way off in the future.

Behavioural economists call this concept "time inconsistency." When we think about the future we want to make decisions that lead to long-term benefits (like starting a savings plan), but when we consider the here-and-now, we tend to make decisions that lead to short-term benefits (let's go shopping).

You know it's true. It's a rare occasion indeed when we have some spare cash in our hot little hand and think, "I'll put this into my retirement fund." The payoff of spending money today is immediate and the cost of neglecting to save for retirement won't affect us for years.

Smoking is something that we all know is harmful to our health but having that one cigarette now doesn't seem that bad. Quitting the habit is the single best thing you can do to improve your future chances of not developing lung cancer. Yet smoking is still a habit and at worst, many choose not to kick it or at least agree that they should.

Another example is the use of fossil-fuels around the world. Burn oil and coal now, worry about the environment later! Industry and society needs the electricity, the heating or cooling and the fuels to run our cars but the effects of climate change won't truly reveal itself until decades of damage have been done.

To test this notion that many of us are predisposed to live in the present rather than consider the distant future, professors Todd Rogers, a behavioural scientist and Associate Professor of Public Policy at the Harvard Kennedy School and Max H. Bazerman, Professor of Business Administration at the Harvard Business School and Co-Director of the Center for Public Leadership at the Harvard Kennedy School, conducted a study in 2006, asking participants whether they would enroll in a savings plan that automatically placed two percent of their weekly pay in a savings account.

Two options were devised and each option presented to half the participants of the study group. Almost every participant agreed that saving money was a good idea however, their behaviour proved otherwise.

The first option asked participants to enroll in a savings plan immediately. In this group, only thirty percent of the participants agreed to enroll in the plan.

The second option asked participants to enroll in a savings plan sometime in the future (maybe a year from now). This group had seventy seven percent of participants agreeing to enroll in the plan.

It turns out that in this particular study, like life in general, we know that making sensible decisions about our future is a good thing but the impulse to actually do something about it doesn't appear that critical to us right now, here in the present.

Joseph Ferrari, PhD, is a professor of psychology and Vincent de Paul distinguished professor at DePaul University in Chicago. Ferrari contends that there are three main types of procrastinators. He labels them as the thrill-seeker, the avoider and the indecisive.

Thrill Seekers

Ferrari's research indicates that procrastinators who say they "work best under pressure" are most likely kidding themselves. More likely, they are wasting time and not getting started because they experience a rush or thrill when it comes to a race against the clock.

Avoiders

Avoiders prefer not to learn more about their strengths and weaknesses in various skills. By not making a decision that impacts their own life, they can pass judgment on those who make a bad decision or bask in the glory of a good decision made by somebody else. Either way, they avoid blame.

Indecisives

Perfectionism leads to procrastination. A common reason why people don't finish tasks is their fear of being judged. By trying to get things perfect and causing a delay, indecisives feel that those they believe will seek to judge them will appreciate the effort rather than the result. Ferrari believes that indecisives procrastinate to shift the responsibility from themselves.

SUCCESS AND WEALTH

Looking further into Thomas C. Corley's study of rich and successful people, he describes a major contributor to procrastination as a lack of passion. He writes, "We simply like to do the things we like to do and we put off the things we do not like to do."

If passion and wealth are connected, it comes as no surprise that lack of passion for your career may be at the very heart of your lack of success. According to Gallup, only thirteen percent of US employees are 'engaged' in their jobs or emotionally invested in their work.

Corley states, "Whether you realise it or not, procrastination is a big reason why you are struggling financially in life. It damages your credibility with employers and fellow colleagues at work. It also affects the quality of your work and this affects the business that you or your employer receives from customers, clients and business relationships."

Napoleon Hill, eighty years earlier concluded, "People who fail to accumulate money, without exception, have the habit of reaching decisions, if at all, very slowly and of changing these decisions quickly and often." – Essentially, they procrastinate.

Of course, it comes as no surprise that procrastination is the archenemy of the emergency manager. In this realm, the future outcomes are generally more dire than retirement savings not being as bountiful as we would have liked. Lives are often at stake and there's nothing like those high-stakes to focus us on the present with clear future outcomes in mind.

ALRIGHT, SO WHAT CAN WE DO ABOUT ALL OF THIS?

Each day, we are faced with hundreds of decisions big and small, and the option to either take the easy way out and jump at instant gratification, be a thrill-seeker, an avoider or an indecisive or skip temptation and commit to a long-term behaviour.

These decisions end up defining our reality and shaping our success.

If you want to beat procrastination and make better long-term choices, then you have to find a way to make decisions now in the best interests of your future, whether that's a day a week or a year. The good news is that anyone can overcome procrastination — and it's simpler than you may think. Don't be fooled though, procrastination is as big a challenge to those who excel in life as it is for those who do not. Nearly everyone is susceptible to procrastination. Acknowledging it, rolling up your sleeves and tackling it head on it can make all the difference. There are three things that you can do to tackle procrastination.

Make the rewards of long-term behaviour more immediate.

The reason we procrastinate is because our mind wants an immediate benefit. If you can find a way to make the benefits of good long-term choices more immediate, then it becomes easier to avoid procrastination. Dr. Ferrari advises getting your rush differently. For example, instead of relying on the deadline for the rush, take pleasure in doing something well before time. You'll experience the thrill of finishing early. Then celebrate. Ideally, make your reward something that you want and can get now. If you can find a way to make the benefits of good long-term decisions more immediate, then it becomes easier to avoid procrastination. Break big tasks into smaller pieces with shorter deadlines and set up rewards.

Make the costs of procrastination more immediate.

Rely on "to-do" lists. They create firm deadlines. Or set a public deadline or tell a friend of your ambition or goals which means that you now have "accountability partners" to ensure you're sticking to your goals and deadlines. If you are not confident making your deadlines public and you don't have any friends you trust then you can place a penalty on your behaviour. For example, each workout you miss, you'll donate fifty dollars to a charity. There's even an App for that. Try Apps such as 'Lift' from www.coach.me, which allows you to use an online community to hold yourself accountable.

Remove procrastination triggers from your environment.

Don't let perfect be the enemy of the good. The first step is to recognise that your quest for perfectionism isn't going to get you any extra points or sympathy.

Dr. Ferrari says that regardless of whether you think you're a perfectionist or not, research shows there is no discernable difference in the way others perceive your delay - you're not going to get sympathy. In other words, labeling yourself a perfectionist doesn't disguise the fact that you're not getting things done.

Unfortunately, personality plays a role in procrastination. Some people are just more impulsive than others. A potent way to change your behaviour is to change your environment. For work, you can block out distractions by going to a quiet location such as a library or restrict yourself from time-wasting internet sites with tools like StayFocusd. At home, your distractions might be TV or food or even your kids. Find a location or set times that you are not to be disturbed. Unplug the TV or avoid the snacks and treats isle at the supermarket next time you do the shopping. It's much harder to procrastinate by bingeing on cookies or chocolates if you don't buy them in the first place.

THE ICING ON THE CAKE

Understanding that very few decisions we make are one hundred percent correct and will remain so is vital in being at ease with our ability to decide. Knowing that we rarely start the process of decision making with all the facts, despite what we may think, is also another thing we need to come to grips with to be at ease with making a decision.

Peter F. Drucker was a writer, professor, management consultant and self-described "social ecologist," who explored the way human beings organise themselves and is perhaps best known for his groundbreaking book, "The Effective Executive – The Definitive Guide to Getting the Right Things Done."

In this book, Drucker describes making effective decisions as, *"A decision is a judgment. It is a choice between alternatives. It is rarely a choice between right and wrong. It is, at best, a choice between 'almost right' and 'probably wrong' - but much more often a choice between two courses of action neither of which is provably more nearly right than the other."*

Another trait of successful millionaires that Napoleon Hill wrote about in Think and Grow Rich, was that in addition to making decisions quickly and confidently, successful people also change decisions, if and when they need to. However, in contrast to making decisions quickly they changed their decisions slowly, Hill noted.

There's one thing that both Hill and Drucker would agree upon. Adjusting your decision depending upon all the variables that may affect that which you have decided upon is vital in ensuring that your decisions are appropriate. This may be by monitoring the outcome of your first actions derived from your initial decision or it may be that additional information has come to light, the circumstances have changed or you have consulted more widely. Asking the right questions is one thing but listening, interpreting and understanding the answers is an important component in any feedback loop. We'll look at feedback loops in later chapters. For now though, to become a better decision maker, start by focusing on your listening skills.

Each of us is born with two ears and one mouth and so, it is a wise person that does twice as much listening as talking.

To arrive at decisions promptly, keep your eyes and ears wide open (and as we'll find out in later chapters, your other senses as well) and your mouth shut. Those who talk too much do little else. If you talk more than you listen, you deprive yourself of the opportunity to gain insights into the very choices upon which you're trying to decide.

I'm going to leave the final word to Napoleon Hill. *"Those who reach decisions promptly, definitely know what they want and they generally get it. The world has the habit of making room for the man whose words and actions show that he knows where he is going."*

THINK – How are procrastination, worry or anxiety affecting you and those around you?

DECIDE – Analyse what's blocking you from making decisions and choose to put some of the recommendations into practice.

ACT – Free your 'physic RAM' by implementing the strategies appropriate to you and beat procrastination. Make your future more certain and successful with decisiveness. Listen more than you talk.

Chapter 2

REMOVE AND SIMPLIFY

"Simplicity is the ultimate sophistication."

- Leonardo da Vinci

Chapter 2 - REMOVE AND SIMPLIFY

In the midst of an emergency is there enough time to develop contingencies and weigh up alternatives? On a rare occasion maybe, but generally the answer is, no. The same is true for available resources. Do you have *enough* information? Is there *enough* equipment available or do you have the *staff* you need to respond or assist? Being ready for any unpredictable event at any moment is a not a regular business activity unless your business *is* emergency management.

The same goes for each of us on a personal level. Have you ever been annoyed when you get a call from a sales and marketing company without warning and they try to get you to decide on switching home loan providers or electricity suppliers? These are all decisions that shouldn't be made in the heat of the moment and yet tele-marketers often use techniques to put pressure on you to decide there and then. They create a sense of urgency with special rates or deals that will expire very soon and you'll miss the opportunity if you don't decide now. They are creating a small-scale emergency situation and trying to use it to their advantage.

This is the point where emergency planning sets the foundation for alternatives. Planning, carried out in advance of an emergency identifies the range of vulnerabilities most likely to affect an organisation or a building and then develops not only a range of actions that should reduce or eliminate the effects of the emergency but also the resources required to perform those actions.

On a personal level, this very same approach can save you from being surprised by even some of life's most basic emergencies. Yes, I know this can be taken to extreme. I am not going to advocate that you should have a bomb shelter built in the back yard or that you should stockpile ninety days worth of food which might see you through Armageddon - although if you've already done that then consider yourself well prepared and you can skip this next part of the chapter!

For those of us without a fully implemented Armageddon strategy, you do probably already take some precautions or plan for adversity without even thinking about it. It has become a habit. Ever taken an umbrella somewhere because 'it looks like rain' or given a helpful hint to a spouse or friend to "Bring a coat, it might be cold"? This is your innate planning at work. Whether you realise it or not, you are planning for *potential* circumstances and forearming yourself with the perceived resources that should solve the problem (emergency) should it arise.

THE HABIT OF PLANNING OR PLANNING A HABIT

I mentioned before that these small measures that many of us take as a matter of course, are *habits.* Do you have a friend or relative who seems to flounder from one emergency to another? Have you ever sat there listening to them describe their latest disaster and think that perhaps they bring it upon themselves or perhaps if they'd had some foresight it shouldn't have happened in the first place? Generally speaking, these are people whose habit of thinking ahead or habit of gathering potential resources isn't that strong.

Again, don't get me wrong here. If you were to plan for every conceivable eventuality that could happen to you in any given day and amassed the resources to deal with them all, two things would probably happen. Firstly, you'd probably never get out of the house for the amount of time you'd need to plan and secondly, you'd need a semi-trailer full of equipment, just in case. Perhaps a secret third thing might happen too - your relatives might demand that you see a psychologist.

By building upon your already existing habits, you can strengthen your ability to have foresight for the resources that you may need. All of us have the ability to create or modify our behaviour if we choose to do so. Motivating yourself and trying to remember a new behaviour is arguably the wrong way to go about it though. Sometimes you'll feel like it and sometimes you won't.

Building upon habits you already have in conjunction with a reminder as the trigger for your new behaviour, is an easy way of forming new habits. A good reminder makes it easier for you to start your habit by associating your new behaviour with something that you already do.

For example, if you wanted to get into the habit of taking an umbrella with you when you walk to work, you might try leaving it next to the front door. Assuming you leave via the front door each morning, this means that the umbrella is there in front of you each time you leave.

Setting up a visible reminder and linking the new habit with one makes it much easier to adopt. It doesn't rely on motivation and by being right there, it doesn't take up our 'psychic ram' having to remember to do it. It's a rare case indeed when any one of us can continuously stick to a new habit without setting up a system that makes it easier to adopt. The reminder that you should use to initiate your new behaviour will be specific to you and the habit that you're trying to create.

Emergency service personnel use a similar method to streamline their response to an emergency. Firefighters, for instance, generally have the habit of 'bunking their boots and overpants' next to the fire appliance. That may be an unusual term so let me explain. Firefighters usually have large, thick fireproof overpants fitted with suspenders that are put on over the day-to-day trousers that they wear around the fire station as part of their uniform. Putting these trousers on over a pair of trousers you're already wearing isn't that easy, especially inside a moving vehicle. Just as difficult is then trying to put on a pair of boots so they slip inside each leg of the overpants. To counter the problem, most, if not all, firefighters when removing the overpants push them down so that they bunch up around the boots they wear to emergencies and then step out of the boots leaving what could be described as – their boots wearing their overpants! The next time the alarm rings and firefighters run to the fire appliance, they simply kick off their shoes, step each foot into their boots, reach down and pull up the overpants and slip the braces over their shoulders.

This strategy is almost a universal convention among firefighters but it is rarely taught in recruit training as a procedure. Recruits pick up the habit from their more experienced peers.

The fire appliance is something that firefighters always take to an emergency (constant) and the boots and overpants next to the appliance should always be worn (association) and the habit of placing the boots 'bunked' in front of the fire appliance door means that when and how to put on the firefighting overpants is done by habit.

But let's get back to dealing with our own cognitive distribution that I spoke of earlier. We can begin to see that our 'physic ram' can start to be freed of worrisome issues simply by forward thinking and a little planning in advance. Don't worry, in coming chapters we'll discuss how to apply emergency decision making to situations or problems we didn't plan for or see coming.

Right now though, what habits could you put in place to reduce or remove having to make a decision, thus freeing yourself from the anxiety of constant decision making? One of the things that can make a dramatic impact upon our mental state is the concept of decision fatigue.

REMOVE AND SIMPLIFY

A simple way to explain decision fatigue is to imagine that you have one hundred one dollar bills in your wallet or purse each day. Every time you make a decision, it costs you a dollar. So, each morning you decide what spread you'll have on your toast, cha-ching - a dollar spent. What shoes shall I wear today? - another dollar spent. Which aftershave today? Which tie or blouse shall I wear? Shall I take lunch to work or eat out today? Cha-ching - three more dollars spent. The decisions go on. It's not hard to imagine that you may have spent fifty dollars of your imaginary one hundred dollars before your day has really even begun in earnest.

Studies on decision fatigue have indicated that in the business environment across all different industries and corporate sectors, decisions made in the afternoon are less effective than decisions made in the morning. Further studies have also concluded that afternoon meetings arrive at less effective decisions or arrive at a decision much slower than meetings conducted in the morning and are much more likely to result in a delayed decision. That means that the decision was not made at all.

This phenomenon of decision fatigue is not the result of the time of day. Afternoon lethargy is a widely recognised human frailty. So much so, that the Spanish have a word for succumbing to the afternoon sleepiness. They call it 'siesta.' Rather than try to push through the effects of afternoon fatigue they go with it, don't fight it and just have a nap. Whilst many of us have experienced the sleepy after lunch feeling, it is usually the result of eating lunch that brings on the afternoon sleepiness. Digestion makes an impact on our blood sugar levels and in dealing with the rigours of digestion and a rise in blood sugar level accompanied by insulin being released into the blood stream to return blood sugar level to normal, we feel the effects of all this biological action in the form of tiredness. Recall the last time you indulged in a festive meal or celebration and how tired you felt a short time afterwards.

Other studies have indicated that towards the end of their shift, shift workers also suffer from the same effects. By analysing shift work and correlating the results with studies of regular –nine to five workers helps determine that decision fatigue is due to the length of time a person is fulfilling a prescribed function (their job) as well as how demanding the task or role is (how many decisions are required to continue the function) rather than the actual time of day the fatigue sets in.

So, without getting too biological or psychological it is a commonly accepted fact that decision fatigue is a valid problem that decision makers must overcome.

One method for tackling decision fatigue head-on is to ensure that crucial decisions, the big decisions you face, are made when you are at your highest energy level. For most nine to fivers, that's in the morning, before lunch. Schedule that team meeting or brainstorming session for the morning. If you are a shift worker then schedule that meeting for early in the shift.

On the home front, personal decisions such as which school to send your child to or where should you go on your next vacation or which make and model of new car to buy, should also be decided upon when you are fresh and available. Ever had the scenario when your spouse gets home after a hard day's work and you hit them with, "What do you want for dinner honey?" and they say they don't care or don't know or whatever you want? Let's face it, if your spouse can't even decide what to have for dinner then how much mental agility is going to be available to decide on a school for the kids or the features and benefits of a new car and so on.

So, schedule complex decisions, problems that require thought or discussion, for times when you're at your freshest. For most of us that is at the beginning of your day's routine.

THE FORCE OF HABIT

I spoke previously about creating and reinforcing new habits. This is the next weapon in our arsenal to combat decision fatigue. Emergency service specialists worldwide rely on this tactic especially, to enhance their emergency response capabilities.

During my firefighting career, every general-purpose fire appliance I rode on was fitted out in an almost identical manner. This ensured that all firefighters from all shifts and all stations could easily swap from one appliance to another and not need any additional training. Even as appliances (fire engines in plain English) changed models, every effort was made to ensure that the new fire appliance was fitted out in as identical a manner as possible to the model it was replacing.

Standardisation in this manner not only allowed the interoperability of firefighters as I mentioned previously, but more importantly specifically catered to the training (habit) of each firefighter. By ensuring that everything remained constant, firefighters could find and operate any piece of equipment located on the appliance even in the dark. No decisions are required as to how to locate a piece of equipment on *this* appliance or how *this* piece of equipment works, it's all standard.

Soldiers and police officers rely on the same system for the equipment that they carry with them. A police officer must be able to instantly access their handcuffs or baton or firearm without delay if the need arises. There's no time for fumbling around or searching pockets trying to remember where they put that pair of handcuffs today. So much so, that drawing a baton in the right circumstance becomes a habit derived from training that seemingly doesn't require a decision. They don't have to think about it, it's just done.

Another example is in the fields of martial arts and combat sports such as boxing. Training in martial arts is designed to hone the athlete's skills to such a point that punches, kicks and other techniques are intuitive rather than the athlete having to stop and think before counter punching or avoiding a knockout blow themselves. Their skills become a habit, built to the point of unconscious competence. Legendary martial artist Bruce Lee once described what he considered to be the height of martial art skills as, *"To truly master form, is to be free of form,"* meaning that a practitioner will practice techniques and hone their skills to the point that they no longer have to conform to rigid rules and make individual decisions on how they react. They just do it.

So how do you harness this power of habit to banish decision fatigue and enhance your decision making abilities? Standardisation to the point where the action is a habit, that's how.

By relegating some of our everyday decisions to unconscious habits we relieve ourselves of decisions. Each decision we don't have to make leaves one of our imaginary dollars in our wallet to spend later on more valuable and worthy decisions. And it doesn't have to be difficult. As the Roman poet Horace once said, *"Don't think. Just do."*

President Barack Obama once explained how he has only a few suits and a small range of ties. Therefore, the choice of what to wear tomorrow is simplified. The President isn't spending his decision-dollars (which might even be considered taxpayer decision-dollars) on trivial decisions like which shirt and which tie to wear to the Oval Office each day. I think you'll agree that you want the person with their finger on the United States nuclear arsenal to be clear of mind and able to make tough and timely decisions if the need arises and certainly not fatigued to the point of indecision or procrastination.

Imagine if President John F Kennedy was informed that missiles had been launched during the Cuba missile crisis and his reply was, "I'm too tired for this, put it in my in basket and I'll deal with it in the morning."

On a much smaller scale but a similar example is that of my wife. Each night she will come home from work and upon entering the house, put her car and house keys somewhere different. Because of the lack of habit or standardisation of this simple practice she regularly wastes time the next time she goes to leave the house and fills her 'physic ram' with recounting her steps trying to recall where she may have put her keys this particular time. I wish I had a dollar for every time I have stood at the front door as we are about to leave and she realises she hasn't got her keys and begins the hunt throughout the house.

Aside from the needless waste of time, the stress this creates prior to leaving the house can have an impact. The cure to remove the decision of what to do with your keys upon returning home is extremely simple and varied. How you choose to standardise this simple example is up to you, as there's no right or wrong method, but the cure is to standardise to such a point that it becomes an unconscious habit that doesn't need to be thought about.

My suggestion to my wife (you know I love you honey) was to use The Big Bang Theory system. Those of us who have enjoyed the popular television sitcom, The Big Bang Theory, will recall that every time that the characters Sheldon or Leonard come home to their apartment, there is a bowl next to the door which they drop their keys into. It's a habit. Guess where their keys are when they need them prior to leaving? Certainly not in the bathroom, under the bed, on the coffee table or, the best one yet, in the freezer!

THINK – Tackle big or complex decisions when your energy is at its highest and remember that decision fatigue is real, which can lead to poor or delayed decisions.

DECIDE – To reduce the number of daily decisions.

ACT – Reducing the number of decisions can be as simple as standardising practices and creating habits.

Chapter 3

NOT EVERY EMERGENCY IS A FIRE

"Failing to plan is planning to fail."

- Benjamin Franklin

Chapter 3 - NOT EVERY EMERGENCY IS A FIRE

I mentioned in the previous chapter that planning positions us so that we avoid situations that require decisions or helps us identify things that we could standardise and relegate to the realm of a 'habit,' resulting is us not having to decide what to do.

Emergency planning ensures that there is a repository of preselected actions or responses for a given type of emergency. If you are in the process of conducting emergency planning for your business, building or organisation, the involvement of other stakeholders in the process is a wise move. At this level it is prudent to have plans and procedures written down.

If you're planning on a personal level, as we spoke of in the last chapter, then your plans don't need to be a physical book or file on a laptop that you constantly carry around with you. It could be simply thinking ahead through the range of scenarios, depending upon what your daily life entails. If you are planning for a possible emergency, then it would be prudent to think about the worst case scenarios that you might encounter.

An example of which may be planning for a long drive in the family car to see relatives interstate. Worst case scenarios include, breakdown or vehicle accident, a medical issue whilst driving between towns or cities or simply running out of fuel. None of these concerns are unique or outlandish and many of us would give them some thought without considering it 'planning.' Those of us who don't consider it planning have developed the habit of foresight.

My father used to have a routine prior to any family vacation that involved a significant road-trip. He'd check all the car's tyres, including the spare in the trunk. He'd then check the oil and radiator and top up if required. I also recall that he'd ensure a small toolbox and a first aid kit were packed as part of our holiday preparations. Was my father a worrywart or person that expected doom and gloom? Absolutely not. It was just a precaution that made sure the inconvenience of a breakdown didn't become a problem or even an emergency because of a little planning in advance.

Will plans and procedures provide a step-by-step guide to every conceivable situation that arises? The answer is no. In fact, it is quite rare that an emergency procedure will be an exact match for the variety of situations and decisions that may occur during the course of an emergency.

Many decisions are made during the development of emergency procedures and there are advantages to having made those decisions during the planning process rather than in the midst of an emergency. Emergency services understand this and devote substantial resources into planning to assist or reduce decision making requirements during an incident.

The same goes for our personal approach to life's decisions and unanticipated events that arise in our lives. We cannot anticipate everything but having some 'rules of thumb' available to us makes unforeseen events less of a challenge and decisions easier to come by. For instance, perhaps you will opt to take the train or bus to work if it's raining rather than walk or if you didn't take an umbrella with you when you left home.

Whilst the previous example is perhaps simple and could even be considered trivial, it is a splendid example of heuristic decision making. We'll visit that specifically in coming chapters.

In the meantime though, looking ahead for things that may go wrong or not as expected and the process of planning our response is entirely based upon our individual knowledge and experience.

FOCUS ON REAL POSSIBILITIES – EVEN IF THEY SEEM BORING

This is where Hollywood movies, in combination with the ever increasing supply of twenty-four seven news and its relentless requirement to bring more and more sensational news to the public, has some explaining to do. In the quest for ratings domination and the sponsorship dollar in the form of advertising, single events that are sensational outrank more commonplace events in most news agencies – even if they're not *that* sensational.

What many people look at when planning ahead may not be entirely correct in terms of what they may actually be at risk from or should be planning for.

High-profile emergencies are like shark attacks because they get a lot of press but they do not represent the greatest threats to buildings, organisations or individuals. Did you know that in the United States every year more people are killed by vending machines than are killed by sharks? Neither did I, but the media goes into a feeding frenzy when there's a shark attack.

Of course, if you are reading this prior to heading out surfing or scuba diving then the threat of a shark attack is more relevant for you and should be taken into account. However, the vast majority of the population in different countries around the world is not swimming in the ocean daily and therefore not at risk from shark attack.

In my career as an emergency management consultant, I've been asked many-a-time how people should respond to an aircraft hitting their building or what the response to a tsunami should be or "What do we do if (insert latest media grabbing emergency) happens here?"

Whilst the concerns *are* worth thinking about, after all if you don't learn from current and past events you're wasting an opportunity, too many people tend to worry too much about high-profile emergency events, when the real threat comes from more mundane, everyday vulnerabilities.

To illustrate this point, the yearly risk (in the United States) of dying from a shark attack is roughly one in two hundred and fifty million, compared to dying from a vending machine accident, which is one in one hundred and twelve million or twice the death rate, whether it's from electrocution or from the machine falling on top of them. Let me know if you've read more on the subject.

Nonetheless, many people live in fear of terrorists, major skyscraper fires, earthquakes, tsunamis and more recently, sinkholes opening up and swallowing them or their building but they do not even blink at the real everyday threats in their home or workplace, such as that sinister vending machine in the hallway.

One of the potential pitfalls that emergency service personnel face is to assume a situation is as they believe it is or it first appears to be. Law enforcement personnel must be constantly aware of stereo-typing or jumping to conclusions. Police, and especially investigating detectives, must keep an inquisitive yet open mind about how things appear, what information eyewitness accounts contain and a host of other underlying factors as to why people may lie or have a skewed recollection of events.

Police investigators, fire cause investigators and even paramedics can make mistakes by having preconceived opinions or being swayed by popular misconceptions. This pitfall is commonly referred to as confirmation bias.

AN OPEN MIND IS AN EFFECTIVE MIND

Wikipedia describes confirmation bias as the tendency to search for, interpret, favour and recall information in a way that confirms one's beliefs or hypotheses, while giving disproportionately less consideration to alternative possibilities.

A relative of confirmation bias is the 'focusing effect.' This is when people concentrate their efforts on one aspect of an event and fail to recognise other factors. So, rather than actively seeking selective information to confirm our point of view, the focusing effect means that we selectively disregard information that may help us interpret a situation more accurately and arrive at a better, more considered decision.

An example of the focusing effect occurred when psychologists asked, "How much happier is a Californian than a Midwesterner?" to residents of both areas. Psychologists were intrigued when the majority of respondents from both locations said that Californians are much happier.

Analysis of survey results in isolation rather than in comparison of 'happiness,' shows that there is no difference between the actual happiness rating of Californians and Midwesterners. Respondents were focusing on the sunny weather in California and the easy-going lifestyle as the leading factors in happiness when actually there are quite a few, lesser-known aspects of happiness that Midwesterners enjoy such as low crime, a lower cost of living, few if any earthquakes and a slower more relaxed pace of life.

Marketers and advertising make heavy use of the focusing effect by convincing customers of the necessary features of a product or service. And it probably comes as no surprise that oftentimes, politicians use focusing to exaggerate the importance of particular issues.

To counter the focusing effect, look at problems from a variety of angles and consider a range of factors before making a decision. By not falling victim to this form of tunnel vision, you are more likely to devote your decision making energy to the things that matter.

So enjoy the latest Hollywood blockbuster for the entertainment it is intended to be and keep abreast of what is going on in the world and locally via your preferred news medium. However, keep an open mind when it comes to some of the descriptions that the media relies on to sensationalise their story above those of rival networks because it can influence the decisions you make about, ...well, nearly everything.

GOOD FORESIGHT BEATS *GREAT* HINDSIGHT

Having the ability to look forward and imagine the most probable decisions you'll face for any given situation is a valuable thing. I used an example in the last chapter of taking an umbrella with you because it looked like rain. To many of us, this seems more like some common sense rather than actual planning. The problem with common sense though, is that it's not that common.

Emergency service personnel have to develop a unique ability to envisage what may happen next during emergencies. They must possess good foresight. Can you imagine if paramedics administer a drug or treatment without some idea of what symptoms indicate that the drug or treatment is working or what adverse reactions the patient may succumb to or perhaps if firefighters did not consider the combination of fire-load, terrain and wind direction when tackling a wildfire in open grasslands? These are both recipes for trouble.

It's always a good thing being able to anticipate something but you don't need to be a clairvoyant. Although if you are a bona fide clairvoyant you're already well ahead of the game and you probably already knew about this chapter before reading it. For the rest of us mere mortals, the ability of good foresight doesn't have to be perfect. The fact that you are thinking ahead means that you're in a good position to avoid making rushed decisions. Therefore, as a situation develops you have less chance of being taken by surprise and constantly playing catch-up.

This is the value of planning. It sets out what needs to be achieved and basically how to achieve it meaning that many of the decisions have been examined and selected as the optimum choice for the envisaged problem prior to the situation happening.

STANDARD OPERATIONAL PROCEDURES

Known as SOPs to the majority of people that abide by them and use them in industry, business, the military and emergency services. Standard Operational Procedures are the result of planning for the most foreseeable set of scenarios most likely to occur. Of course, this is going to vary dramatically based upon what industry or activities any person or organisation is engaged in but for all organisations, they are both necessary and useful. However, SOPs are extremely flawed unless coupled with a level of intrinsic knowledge from those expected to abide by the procedures.

The benefit of strict procedures is that they are applicable in set circumstances. That is to say that it is easy to follow a procedure when the circumstances do not change. Some examples you may be familiar with include a vehicle service manual or the included instructions on how to assemble some IKEA furniture (or perhaps not!) because the furniture is mass produced and the parts and assembly method are identical for each unit of each piece of furniture. There are few, if any, variables.

However, all procedures assume a working knowledge by the end user. The last set of assembly procedures that I saw from IKEA did not provide instructions as to which end of the screwdriver to hold and which end is used on the screw head and which way to rotate the screw to assemble part A with part B etc. It made the assumption that I knew what a screwdriver was and how to use it.

When I speak to groups regarding emergency procedures I often use the following example to highlight how important it is to understand the emergency plan and the accompanying procedures. Yet this example highlights how rigid adherence to procedures can often be counterproductive.

I often ask groups if they can envisage writing a set of step-by-step procedures for riding a bicycle. After all, there are so many things in this world that are described as 'Simple – like riding a bike' or 'It's like riding a bike. Once you learn you never forget.' Most groups agree that bike riding basics could be listed one by one and instruct the learner to sit on a bike, where to put their feet, which way to push the pedals and how to control the handlebars and steer the bike but the exercise comes to a sudden halt when the procedures for balancing on a two-wheeled bike need to be included.

I then ask the audience to imagine that they have never ridden a bicycle and ask for a show of hands from those in the room who believe that after reading the instructions they would know *how* to ride a bike.

Then I ask for a show of hands from those who believe that after reading the instructions they *could* ride a bike.

If you're like most participants who have taken part in this exercise, many of you would feel confident that the instructions give you the required knowledge of *how* to ride a bike but there's seldom anyone with their hand still raised when I ask who thinks that by reading our instructions they *could* ride a bike.

That's because we all know that there is a level of personal experience and skill that is required in order for each of us as individuals to balance on a bicycle. We each act, react, feel and perceive the experience of balancing on a bicycle differently, despite the outcome being the same.

If you've never ridden a bicycle or assembled IKEA furniture then there's one other example you might be familiar with. In the movie, 'A Few Good Men' starring Tom Cruise, Demi Moore and Jack Nicholson, Tom Cruise's character is Lieutenant Daniel Kaffee, a navy lawyer assigned to defend two US marines being court-marshalled after the death of a fellow marine, Private First Class Santiago. Santiago's death is allegedly due to them administering some rough treatment to the now deceased marine. This 'rough treatment' was known by the term as a 'code red.'

In one scene, the prosecuting legal counsel hands one of the two defendants in the witness box a copy of the US Marine Corp field manual and asks if the manual contains everything a marine needs to know and how to do it. The answer is "Yes." The prosecuting counsel than asks the marine to turn to the section entitled 'Code Red' to which the defendant is cornered into admitting that there is no section or instructions for a 'code red' in the manual. Clearly, the defendants have acted outside the code of conduct of the US Marine Corp.

To counter the argument that not absolutely everything is contained within the US Marine Corp field manual, LT Kaffee (Tom Cruise) takes the very same field manual and asks the defendant to turn to the section that instructs marines how to find the mess hall. Of course, there are no instructions and the defendant is asked, "How then, does a marine manage to find the mess hall and feed himself if the instructions are not in the manual?" Answer: "I just follow the other marines to the mess hall sir." Clearly, not absolutely everything can become a set-in-stone procedure, even in the US Marine Corp.

These examples show us that whilst procedures can prescribe specific steps to achieving an outcome, they are most beneficial when combined with a level of tacit knowledge or training and applied in set and predictable circumstances.

The moment the circumstances of the situation we are trying to apply procedures to changes, the procedures may become difficult to adhere to or even counterproductive to our endeavours.

Understanding that procedures have limitations frees us to apply our observation skills and problem-solving and decision making abilities to non-routine circumstances.

BREAK THE RULES BUT KEEP THE FAITH

Without doubt, emergency services make heavy use of procedures. However, they are in the unique position that almost every situation that they attend will differ from the last, even when the emergency may be of a similar or almost identical nature. No two fires are the same, no two vehicle accidents are identical and storms frequently cause trees to collapse onto houses but the recovery and response to each situation will be similar yet different.

These situations are all unique and some may be even described as 'novel.' Novel being used in this context means something not encountered before. A historic example is the World Trade Center attacks in 2001 in New York.

In 1992, I was fortunate enough to do a ride along and hang out with New York firefighters at a station in Manhattan for a few shifts. Australians were rather popular in the US during the early nineties due to the movie Crocodile Dundee. I was on vacation visiting the US and decided to see if I could have a look around a New York fire station whilst I was in Manhattan. When I knocked on the door of the station and introduced myself it was as if I was a long-lost cousin. The guys welcomed me in and gave me coffee and even a meal as well as a grand tour of their station and fire appliances. I am still grateful to this day for their generosity and camaraderie.

I am certain that if I had asked the firefighters if any of them had ever attended an incident involving an airliner hitting one of the skyscrapers in the Big Apple's skyline the answer would have been a resounding no. So too with specific training for or having procedures for such a situation. The events of September 11th 2001 were novel. It was something never encountered at that magnitude before and with any luck something we'll never encounter again.

So, procedures kick start the emergency response but not every action, reaction or tactic can be captured in a procedure. People need procedures to guide their responses but they have to move within or even beyond procedures in order to fully achieve their desired outcome.

By knowing that procedures that are applied to situations that are more fluid than IKEA furniture assembly or changing the fan belt on the family car are limited, means that we can use procedures to better suit our circumstance.

So let's look at a few of the limitations. Once we are aware of the limitations of procedures we can progress with confidence in making decisions that might not comply precisely with your organisation's procedures and how, when dealing with situations that aren't exactly routine, you're equipped to cope.

Procedures alone don't cut it in fluid situations

In dynamic or complex situations we simply cannot write procedures that can predict or contain all eventualities. Even if we tried, I'm confident that the resulting set of procedures would be so comprehensive and unwieldy so as to be almost unusable. Something unexpected will arise or the situation will evolve faster than we can look up, read and action the prescribed procedure.

Procedures can be extremely effective at preventing situations from occurring, for example 'safety-procedures' are routine procedures that can reduce the likelihood of an accident or emergency (non-routine) situation occurring.

Even the everyday situation of riding a bike goes beyond procedures and involves our decision making abilities on numerous levels in combination with our body's senses.

Updating procedures is a challenge

Making sure that procedures keep pace with industry or life in general is difficult. Now, more than ever, the rate at which software is developed or new ideas, products and services hit the market is increasing.

Uber is shaking up the taxi and transport industry. Many countries are still debating the legality of Uber months, if not years, after the service has become available. Airbnb is a similar game-changer in the tourism, hotel and hospitality industry. Regulators the world over are furiously trying to keep pace with rules, regulations and laws that take these services and more into account and consequently the procedures for how these services will be implemented, governed and controlled are also lagging.

Because procedures take time to catch up or evolve to match circumstances, people develop their own workarounds to cope with outdated or cumbersome procedures. In Australia, at present Uber is legal in some states but not in others but I know of many people who have used the service despite it currently being deemed illegal.

Procedures may make you a robot

Having procedures to follow can lull people into a zombie like state in that they just follow the steps without any actual thought. Whilst this may be beneficial in a few situations, it leads to people switching off and oftentimes this is when accidents happen. Think of a time when you had an accident and it was the result of you just 'not thinking.' Don't worry, we've all done it.

This zombie like state also has the effect of lowering our motivation for the given tasks or job and may even lead to high employee turnover as people develop the 'what's the point' attitude and seek different employment.

Endless procedures can wear you down

Lack of motivation may also inhibit improvement or updating of the procedures due to lack of interest from those entrusted to use the procedures. Expertise in an organisation may diminish due to motivated engaged employees seeking alternative employment elsewhere and lethargic non-motivated employees staying put.

Studies have highlighted that people do best when they understand what it is they are doing and why. Essentially, if people know what they are doing and doing what they know then they are much more capable of dealing with a situation when something goes wrong or is non-routine.

So, a plan may tell us what we're setting out to achieve and procedures can tell us the steps towards achieving it but the implementation and application is entirely an individual contribution. As I mentioned previously, a plan doesn't always have to be as formal as a written manual but a plan that involves others that is not shared is doomed.

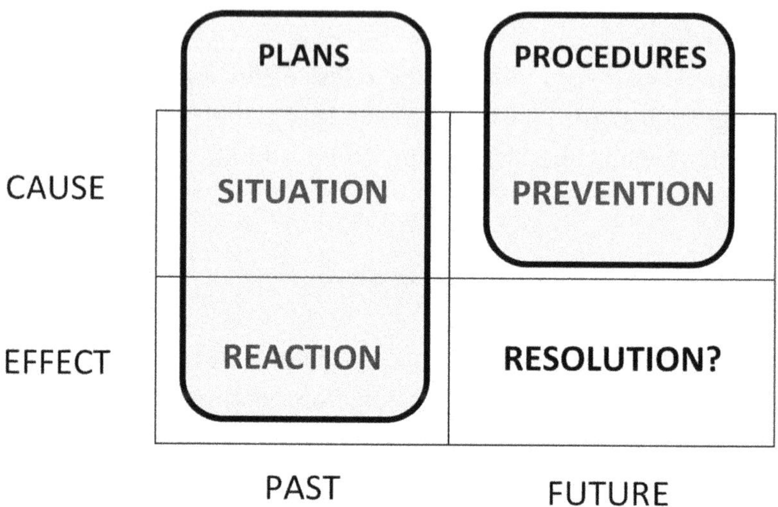

A PROBLEM SHARED IS A PROBLEM HALVED

It's also important to understand that the planning process is more important than the plan itself. This is because there is a different level of comprehension between developing and understanding a procedure to deal with a problem, than finding and learning a procedure at the time you need it. Looking forward and determining if a procedure will contend with an emergency ensures readiness rather than assessing a procedure that was poorly constructed and looking back to find out why it was so inadequate.

For example, during my career as an emergency management consultant, I've encountered many a client who waits patiently whilst I examine their facility, interview staff, inspect emergency warning systems and equipment and analyse the risks inherent in their operational environment. Then, perhaps weeks later, when I deliver a customised emergency response procedures manual, the client is elated at the results.

What generally happens next is the amazing part. The glossy new emergency procedures manual is placed on a shelf in the manager's office to take pride of place next to other compliance documentation, booklets and manuals.

To my client's mind, the manual needs to be on hand if the facility is audited by safety inspectors or building auditors. That's quite often the end result of all the diligent analysis and work that went into its compilation. Where is the manual when an emergency strikes? Who knows? Not in the hands of the person entrusted to act on behalf of the facility when the pressure is on.

You already know this to be true and it's probably happened to you at some time or other. Recall a time when a friend explained a plan to get together on the weekend or a travel itinerary for a holiday. Unless you were part of the planning process you take on board only key points of the plan, the rest is seemingly unimportant detail. For instance, your friend intends to pick you up on Saturday to drive you to lunch at an amazing restaurant that has an award-winning menu, stunning views and quirky waiters. Your friend has warned you that the traffic can be bad in the afternoon in that part of town, let alone finding somewhere to park the car and so on and so on. What are you most likely to remember about the arrangements (plan)?

Probably key points like, friend; pick up; be ready by midday.

If you are putting together contingencies for your business or organisation, it's worth remembering that a plan accomplishes nothing. Endeavours succeed or fail on the abilities of people to enact that plan. This relies on them knowing what to do and how to do it.

Having a plan is one thing. Having a plan that people know about, can follow and have had some training in the procedures that the plan advocates, is something else entirely.

By taking part in the planning process, everyone has an insight into the formation of procedures, it creates awareness of the procedures and most importantly, it promotes buy-in from those very people that the plan and procedures seeks to involve.

BUY-IN

This is an insight I learned at a young age and the manner in which it was brought to my attention was unusual but it stays with me to this day. As an adolescent many years ago now, I saw an interview on television conducted by Michael Parkinson or 'Parky' as he was affectionately known the world over. He was interviewing Sir Paul McCartney of The Beatles fame.

During the course of the interview, Parky asked a question that perhaps only Parky could get away with because of his gentle and trustworthy demeanor. He asked Sir Paul about his reputation for being 'tight' with his money despite being (at the time) the richest man in Britain. If memory serves me, I recall the audience drawing breath and going very quiet, perhaps waiting for McCartney to let fly with a rebuttal of some kind.

However, McCartney carefully considered the question and agreed with Parky that he was indeed careful with money and that growing up poor had taught him the value of wealth. Parky pushed a little more by recounting a story of how McCartney made his young daughter Stella earn pocket money by doing household chores.

McCartney conceded that the story was one hundred percent true and that he does indeed make Stella clean the house and do other tasks despite having a veritable troop of staff such as butlers and maids. He then proceeded to explain it like this:

"*My children must come to value what they have. This is my method of making them appreciate what they have. For instance, when John (Lennon) and I were young, our first few music gigs earned us enough money to buy a Morris 1000. We loved that car. We fixed it up. We polished it each week and it saw us through the fledgling years until we teamed up with George and Ringo.*"

McCartney continued, "*Contrast that however, with nowadays when my chauffeur a week ago now, came into the house to inform me that my new custom made Bentley had just arrived and asked if I would like to come outside and inspect it. To which I replied, Nah, just park it round the back and I'll look at it later!*"

McCartney concluded that, "*If my kids don't work to get something they'll never value it, just like me and the Bentley. I don't want that to happen so I ensure that they don't get everything they want every time they want it.*"

Now, this is not a parenting book and you may be wondering what this has to do with planning but simply put, if your planning is done *for* you, you have no buy-in to what it contains or how it works. However, if you have to work a little, and have input, you value that emergency plan more and you are intimate with its contents.

EVEN THE BIG GUNS CAN GET IT WRONG

I mentioned at the outset of this chapter that if you are in the process of conducting *emergency* planning for your business, facility or organisation, the process and the involvement of other stakeholders is a wise move. When planning for business, buildings or organisations that are worth tens of thousands of dollars, if not millions, you could be forgiven for expecting that emergency planning is a routine and professional undertaking where every conceivable vulnerability is assessed and addressed.

Unfortunately, that is not always the case and some famous examples of shortcomings in emergency planning involved not only financial losses but tragic loss of life as well. For example, the international airline industry spans the globe and nowadays has so many airplanes in the air simultaneously that there is not enough space in all the airports around the world for all these planes to be grounded. This was a realisation that came to light during the historic September 11, World Trade Centre attacks and subsequent grounding of every flight in US airspace.

In the fifteen years since this catastrophic event you, like I, would have assumed that the business of international air travel and flight management has made tremendous improvements in air safety, security, air traffic control and search and rescue should the worst happen. By and large we'd be correct. Technology has certainly gone ahead in leaps and bounds. However, there's still room for some of the most basic errors to continue to happen.

For instance, part of good foresight is developing a relationship with your neighbours. Emergencies do not stop at defined borders, whether that is globally between countries, between state borders, between neighbouring properties or at walls between tenants within the same building. Emergencies are random and indiscriminate.

The mystery of Malaysian Airlines flight MH370 is a prime example of failure to communicate. MH370 was an international passenger flight that disappeared on the 8th of March, 2014 while flying from Kuala Lumpur, Malaysia to Beijing in China.

Society at large, myself included, presumed that the global aviation industry had long-standing agreements and systems to address international air travel and air safety. Previous aviation incidents have demonstrated how professional search and rescue capabilities are within navies, air forces and coast guards around the globe. So then, how did the search for a large commercial aircraft such as flight MH370 become such a fiasco?

Lack of foresight to establish relationships and communication channels.

After the incident, Malaysia's allies and neighbours did not share satellite information in a timely fashion. China took three days to release its pictures of debris in the South China Sea. It took four days for Australia to reveal images taken by a US satellite of large flotsam in the southern Indian Ocean. Thailand didn't share its knowledge that it picked up what may have been MH370 on its radar for ten days, saying they were never asked. The Vietnamese claim that they were sent to search the wrong area by the Malaysians.

Relatives of the passengers were demanding answers and were receiving a different story each time they asked. This mess funnelled into bad communication practices and a gross failure to talk with neighbouring countries to discuss planning for and cooperation in, such circumstances *before* they became a reality.

Perhaps the fate of MH370 will come to light one day but the flight's fate is not really what we're focusing on in this book. What is of interest to us is that communication and involvement is the key to good planning.

THINK – A plan sets out your desired outcomes. Procedures are how you'll achieve them.

DECIDE – Procedures are useful in set routine circumstances but may prove inappropriate in non-routine or novel circumstances.

ACT – Planning in advance gives you time to obtain "buy-in" from the people your plan involves.

Chapter 4

MENTAL SHORT CUTS

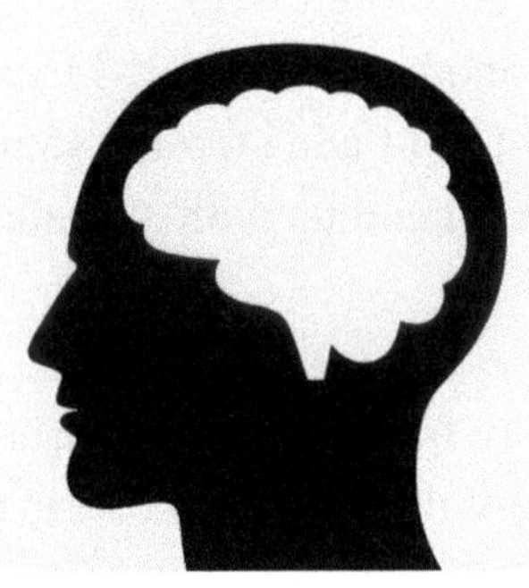

"If a plan isn't perfect but it works, then it's perfect."

- Russell Boon

Chapter 4 – MENTAL SHORT CUTS

Each time I cook a pizza in my oven I don't reach in and grab hold of the pizza tray to remove the cooked pizza and burn my hand. That's because I know that the pizza tray in a hot oven is hot enough to cook a pizza and therefore hot enough to burn me. I simply use an oven mitt to protect my hand. Easy!

I know squinting in bright sunlight gives me a headache. Therefore, before venturing outside on a sunny day I grab my sunglasses and put them on. I have found that the more I wear sunglasses the more I need to wear sunglasses but that's another discussion. I know that my sunglasses shield my eyes from bright light and stop me squinting. Consequently, I can see better and also don't end up with a headache after more than a few minutes outside.

When I go bushwalking with friends I always ensure that I lace my boots firmly to prevent my boots rubbing on the backs of my ankles and giving me blisters. Walking on rough terrain, sometimes for days at a time, can loosen the laces and my boots begin to rub. Blisters are painful and certainly no joy to have if you still have another day of hiking ahead of you. I also ensure that I wear thick socks when I go hiking, even if the weather is warm. The socks add an additional level of protection to my ankles.

By now you are wondering if the publisher has inserted pages from someone else's book. After all, this is supposed to be about decision making forged from emergency service experience. So what am I talking about?

Each of us has 'rules of thumb,' 'tricks of the trade' or other quick fixes for common problems we regularly encounter. Emergency service personnel are no different.

Near one of the fire stations where I spent a portion of my career, was a lower than usual bridge spanning across the road. Quite regularly, once, occasionally twice a year a truck driver would drive under the bridge and find out the hard way that their truck was indeed higher than the bridge clearance and come to a loud and abrupt stop.

The first time I attended an incident like this I was perplexed as to how we'd resolve the situation. The offending vehicle was well and truly wedged under the bridge. The truck had already tried to reverse out from under the bridge but it was immovable. Besides, there was concern that the top of the truck dragging backwards from under the bridge would cause more damage to the bridge, effectively making the situation worse. So, the integrity of the bridge was the main focus of our attention, not the already damaged truck.

By the way, in nearly all the incidents of this type, the driver escaped with minor injuries but always suffered a severe case of embarrassment.

At first, an incident such as this looks to be quite complex and perhaps even costly to fix. Should bridge engineers be called in to assess if the bridge can be dismantled to get the truck out without causing further damage to the bridge? Should the truck be subjected to the 'jaws of life' and become some serious practice for firefighters to cut the truck open and remove sections of the truck's load compartment, allowing it to be removed? The options are many and varied but nine times out of ten the solution was much simpler, more cost-effective and quicker.

Let the tyres down. Deflating the tyres usually decreased the pressure between the roadway and the bridge, allowing the truck to reverse out from under the bridge without causing further damage to the bridge. If the truck was not able to be reversed out under its own power it would be winched out by a tow-truck.

This trick-of-the-trade isn't something that was standard procedure written in any instruction manual and taught at firefighter recruit training school. It's just a handy trick that solves a situation that some emergency service personnel find themselves confronted with. The problem appears complex but the solution seems surprisingly simple.

TRICKS OF YOUR TRADE

Getting pizzas out of the oven, grabbing your sunglasses before venturing down to the beach or preventing blisters when bushwalking or jogging and even retrieving wedged trucks from under low bridges, all rely on tried and tested solutions that may not be perfect but they work.

To get a pizza out of the oven I could buy one of those long paddles that you see at restaurants with wood ovens. Although if you saw how small my kitchen is, that would pose more of a problem than a solution.

To stop me squinting when I'm outside on sunny days I could wear a hat or close my eyes. Both solutions work but I'm confident that closing my eyes isn't the best idea whilst walking or driving!

And to prevent blisters whilst walking long distances I could walk barefoot or wear flip-flops instead of boots. Maybe I could use sticky plaster and tape the back of my ankles before putting my boots on and that way prevent the boot rubbing directly onto my skin.

All these solutions *are* solutions. Some better than others and perhaps the solutions I mentioned are not the optimal 'fix' for the problem, but they work. They are referred to as heuristic and I, like you and emergency service personnel, use heuristic decision making all the time.

HEURISTIC .... WHAT?

If you are like me then you may have first encountered this word via your antivirus scanner on your computer. If you have your propeller hat on and want to investigate some of the deeper settings in your antivirus program (your computer has an anti-virus program right?) then get all 'geeky' and investigate. Somewhere in the settings you'll encounter something like 'Scan computer using heuristics' or a setting that has something like 'Turn on heuristic scanning.'

Mathematicians and computer programmers turn away now whilst I give an extremely simple explanation of heuristic virus scanning.

Commonly, a heuristic analysis in an antivirus program examines your hard drive for suspicious programs that may be lurking within another program or file. Your antivirus program then analyses the source code within that file. The source code of the suspicious file is compared to the source code of known viruses and virus-like activities. If a portion of the source code matches the code of known viruses or virus-like activities, then your program will alert you to a *potential* virus.

A friend once explained this to me as, "Your antivirus scanner is scanning for files it knows are viruses. It (the antivirus program) has a list of viruses it rapidly refers to and compares when assessing if something is a virus or not. Heuristic scanning however, is where your antivirus might not know what virus it has detected but it can detect the shadow of virus like activity, essentially alerting you to something on your computer that doesn't pass the 'sniff-test'."

Anyway, enough of the computer geek-speak, you can take off your propeller-hat now.

Heuristic is an ancient Greek word meaning to 'find' or 'discover.'

Heuristic methods often referred to as just 'a heuristic,' approaches problem solving by employing a practical solution that may not be optimal or perfect but is sufficient for a satisfactory outcome.

HEURISTIC DECISION MAKING

Back in Chapter 2 I used the example of taking the train or bus to work if it's raining rather than walk or if you didn't take an umbrella with you when you left home. I labeled this simple and quick fix to a problem as a heuristic decision. As I mentioned previously, there's a whole host of other solutions that would save you getting soaked by the rain on the way to work. Rather than anguishing over the decision of which solution is optimal for your current situation you simply go with the easiest to implement in the circumstances you find yourself in and that your experience tells you will work. Catch a bus, take the train, buy an umbrella or simply get wet.

Whether you realise it or not, you made a decision.

A large portion of successfully managing emergencies is having a wide range of rules-of-thumb at your disposal. Firefighters use water on most fires, police officers know handcuffs will restrain most people they arrest and paramedics know that oxygen is beneficial when a patient complains of chest pain.

Where finding an optimal solution is impossible or impractical, heuristic decision making can be used to speed up the process of finding a satisfactory solution.

The decision of paramedics to administer oxygen to a patient that has chest pain is beneficial if the patient is suffering a heart attack but not so effective if the patient has simply strained a muscle or has sustained a bruise to their chest region. However, whilst the patient's condition is diagnosed, heuristic decision making dictates to treat the patient for the worst-case scenario using a method that, whilst not a cure, will mitigate some of the effects of the symptoms.

If the paramedics subsequently diagnose that the patient *is* suffering a heart attack then the initial decision to administer oxygen has already been made and the patient is already receiving an appropriate treatment. The paramedics can continue to provide additional treatment now that the situation is clearer.

In business, heuristic decision making is everywhere and is especially useful in businesses that require fast decisions to be made. Specialty areas such as the stock market, where shares and stocks rise and fall within minutes if not seconds due to global and market forces and the decision to buy, sell or hold is critical, is a good example.

That's not to say that being aware of heuristic decision making suddenly makes you a stock market guru or even a paramedic. I am simply highlighting that we all have a range of mental shortcuts that ease the cognitive load of making a decision.

DON'T LET PERFECT BE THE ENEMY OF THE GOOD

In business and everyday life we encounter novel or unique situations requiring a decision. For most people, they are rarely of the instant, split-second emergency kind. We generally have a little time to gather our thoughts or ask a few questions and gain an insight as to what the best course of action is. That may be a few seconds or perhaps a minute or two.

If the situation is familiar, then we can use heuristics in a speedy fashion. If the situation or problem is unfamiliar then we can still use a rule of thumb, an educated guess, an intuitive judgment, stereotyping, profiling or common sense to get us started and progress us towards making more sense of the situation.

SATISFICING

If we have considered the situation and judged it not to be familiar then the hunt for a solution begins. What will probably happen next, especially if we have a time constraint affecting us, is that we will generally think of or devise a workable solution and implement that.

Our workable solution may not be the best solution and what's even more interesting is that most people will stop generating ideas and options after they come up with the first option they think stands to work. They satisfice. That is, they opt for a satisfactory or adequate result, rather than the optimal solution because trying to find an optimal solution may take unnecessary additional time, energy and resources.

In essence, near enough is good enough. Or to put it another way, good enough is good enough.

WHERE THE RUBBER MEETS THE ROAD

So, reacting to an event that we didn't anticipate or is novel for us requires a decision and action means that we don't have to find the perfect solution immediately. A workable solution that can either solve or partially mitigate the situation until the situation becomes clearer to us is the kick start to making decisions on the fly.

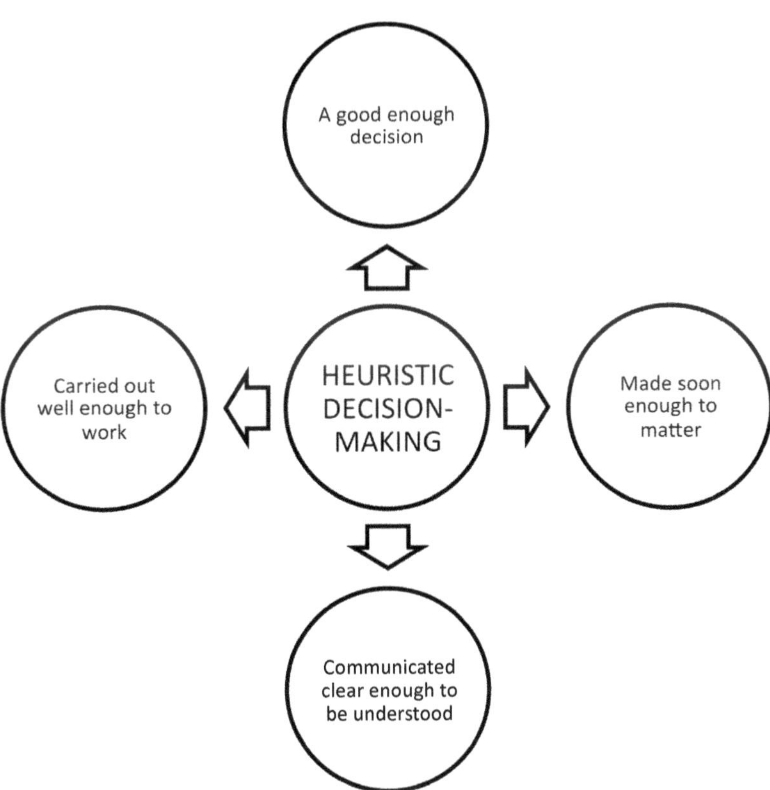

Depending upon the circumstance you find yourself in, heuristics may not be entirely appropriate. Many business decisions require accurate data, consultation and analysis before a decision is made. There is nothing wrong with this form of traditional problem solving and decision making. When time is plentiful and reliable sources of data are available then it is foolhardy to not make use of them.

This is also true with personal situations such as buying a new car, moving house, accepting a new job, choosing a school for your child to attend or whether to buy a Mac or PC. Generally speaking, these decisions are best made with investigation, analysis, contemplation, discussion and in a time and manner acceptable to you.

Heuristics are extremely helpful for the unanticipated situation (emergency) where time is short, data is only partially available and perhaps the situation is somewhat fluid.

HOW IMPERFECT IS GOOD ENOUGH?

Sometimes not getting a decision perfect can work to your advantage. Striving for the perfect decision can slow down our ability to think, decide and act. In situations less critical than life-and-death situations, sometimes less than perfect can be a conduit to an improved relationship with those we share the situation and decision with. That may be your sporting team mates, family, friends or business colleagues.

I discovered this myself in an awkward manner but instead of reflecting negatively on me it turned out to improve my relationship with those who I was interacting with at the time.

Part of the emergency management consultation I offer to my clients is to conduct training sessions. The training sessions are for the people in the facility appointed as emergency wardens. Throughout these sessions I teach the procedures that have been prepared for that particular building and to help facilitate learning I also include a lot of why we are going to respond in the manner being advocated. People always respond better to instructions or follow procedures more closely if they know why things are done in such a manner.

Recently, I was conducting a training session for a large skyscraper in Melbourne, Australia. The building is one of my favourite presentation venues and comes complete with lectern (although I rarely if ever stand behind it) and three projection screens. One large screen is at the front centre stage behind me and two smaller screens to either side, which replicate the larger screen.

On this particular occasion, as the room began filling with attendees, I could not get the audio-visual system to work. This was perplexing as I had used the venue many times previously. Hastily I called the venue 'techies' in to assist me and get my presentation up and running before the advertised start time of the training.

The technical assistants systematically ran through all the tried and tested tricks to get the system up and running, many of which I had tried prior to their arrival. I even tried that stalwart of anything vaguely computer related and rebooted the entire system to no effect, which of course was the first step the assistants used as well. A reboot didn't work for them either.

After two reboots and much 'cable wiggling' the technical assistants scratched their heads and concluded that they were dumbfounded as to the reason why the system was unresponsive. Not good news for me as I was now looking at a lecture theatre with over one hundred people in it and still more people were arriving.

Consequently, I unpacked my portable projector and quickly began plugging it in, balancing it precariously on a chair and using a few hastily resourced books and magazines to elevate and angle the projector at the main screen at the front of the theatre.

After an introduction that started with an apology for the less-than-perfect audio-visual projection I launched into the presentation. In fact, I used the situation to highlight emergency management 101 – do what you can with what you've got right here, right now.

Have you ever had one of those days? If so, you'll know the story doesn't stop there. Half way through the presentation the batteries in my remote control that advances the slides of my presentation went flat. That left me to finish the presentation by walking to the computer each time I needed to advance a slide and pressing a button on the keyboard. Not usually a problem when the computer is on a lectern but balanced on a chair atop of books and magazines, it's a little more tricky and inconvenient.

Needless to say, by the end of the presentation I felt like a complete rank amateur and that I had not performed at my best. A confession that I made to the building's facility manager, to which she replied, "Not at all. In fact it was the ideal manner to demonstrate that things are not always ideal and that even an emergency manager encounters problems." She continued, "In fact, I think it made people feel more connected to you because you didn't come across as perfect but you made the most of it and still got the job done."

And she was right. Attendees thanked me for the training and in doing so I encountered what seemed to be a more personable approach from the people in the session. They didn't feel too intimidated to come and speak with me because I had just demonstrated that I was just like them. Stuff goes wrong for me too and I have to make a decision as to what to do.

I had just become a victim of the Pratfall Effect.

People who never make mistakes are perceived as less likeable than those who make the occasional faux pas. Perfection creates distance and an unattractive aura of invincibility.

The Pratfall Effect is the tendency for attractiveness to increase or decrease after an individual makes a mistake, depending on the individual's perceived competence or abilities.

It was first identified by award winning American psychologist, Elliot Aronson, who published a paper in 1966 describing an experiment that tested the effects of a simple blunder on perceived attraction. In his test, he asked participants to listen to recordings of people answering a quiz. Some of the recordings included the sound of the person knocking over a cup of coffee.

The test subjects were then asked which of the people in the recordings taking the quiz were more 'likable.' When the results were tallied, the majority of participants said that the people who suffered the coffee spill were more likeable.

So perhaps we can take some comfort in that the Pratfall Effect is a reminder that it is okay to be fallible. Occasionally making a mistake is not only acceptable, it may even be beneficial, provided the mistake is not critical and does not compound a reputation for being clumsy or reckless.

THINK - We all have mental shortcuts that we can draw upon to ease our decision making load on a daily basis. We can also apply these shortcuts to situations that are similar to situations we recognise.

DECIDE - Using a heuristic method can help us make sense of a situation and provide clarity leading to a better and more considered decision later on when we have time to reflect upon our decisions and actions.

ACT - Trying to be perfect is a wasteful endeavour and may stagnate our decision making abilities. Also, if our mistakes are noticed, provided the decision was not critical, then it's okay to be less than perfect and quite often good enough is good enough.

Chapter 5

FRAMING

"The way we see a problem is the problem."

- Dr. Steven Covey

Chapter 5 - FRAMING

I mentioned in Chapter 1 that 'framing' can set our decision making off to an awkward start. Framing means how a problem is described and put into context. This plays a significant part in how a problem is first approached.

Frames are mental models that people use to simplify their understanding of the complex world surrounding them. It helps all of us make sense of it. Often taken for granted, these mental models involve our assumptions about how things are. How we frame a problem often shapes the solutions and decisions that we make.

As Oscar Wilde once said, *"The optimist sees the donut, the pessimist sees the hole."*

In their research paper, "The Framing of Decisions and the Psychology of Choice," psychologists Amos Tversky and Daniel Kahneman concluded that framing situations in terms of a loss causes people to take more risks. Their research showed that people act differently if a decision is framed in terms of the probability that lives will be saved, as opposed to lives lost.

Their experiment asked participants to imagine that the USA is preparing for the outbreak of an 'unusual Asian disease' which is expected to kill six hundred people. Two medical programs have been devised to combat the disease. Program A *will* save two hundred lives and yet in Program B there is a one in three chance of saving all six hundred and a two in three chance that no people will be saved.

Seventy two percent of participants opted for Program A, leaving twenty eight percent of participants opting for Program B. As Tversky and Kahneman put it, "The majority choice in this problem is risk adverse: The prospect of certainly saving two hundred lives is more attractive than a risky prospect of equal expected value, that is, a one-in-three chance of saving six hundred lives."

Their work shows that we make different decisions given alternative frames, even if the expected values in both situations are identical.

As we've just seen, the same problem posed to test groups in numerous other scientific studies, consistently concludes that groups will arrive at different solutions depending upon how the problem is described or 'framed.' For instance, you might frame a problem to one group by stating that, 'We can't afford to fail when addressing problem x,' and describe the same problem to the other group as 'How could we improve upon problem x?'

The second manner of posing the need for a solution invites all group members to think freely and discuss ideas that, hopefully, arrives at a decision regarding a recommended solution. The first manner of posing the question causes the group to be very selective in what they propose. They may hesitate regarding a final decision on whether to proceed with a chosen solution.

Framing of a problem doesn't need to be complex. Even the terminology used may present a problem in a different way. This one important factor regarding decision making can even make a lifesaving difference. Take, for instance, the renaming of safety ramps on freeways to arrester beds. Many freeways the world over build arrester beds alongside the freeway at strategic points, particularly if the freeway has a long continuous decline or steep descent. If a heavy vehicle should have its brakes fail, it can pull off the road into an arrester bed, bringing the vehicle to a stop. Basically it is a pit filled with round pebbles that, when the truck drives into the bed of pebbles, will slow its speed dramatically and assist with bringing the vehicle to a safe stop and also if the bed includes a ramp, stop the vehicle from rolling backwards and back onto the freeway. The very same technique is now used on racing car circuits to slow and stop cars that run off the track.

However, improved safety may have resulted in an *increase* of runaway trucks.

How can such improvements result in the opposite effect that was intended? Initial enquiries are alluding to the unwillingness of truck drivers to use an ‘arrester bed,’ preferring to attempt to try and stop their vehicle by other means. Apparently, the term ‘arrester’ plays an important part in the decision making process when dealing with the emergency of a runaway heavy vehicle.

The framing of the emergency solution may have resulted in many more drivers neglecting to use the arrester beds because of the inconvenience of their vehicle being arrested by the pebble beds and the inability for them to repair their truck and continue on their way. Instead, they will require towing out of the arrester bed, which will incur costs and increase any delay they may suffer.

In a business where time is money, delays such as this are costly and certainly not something any truck driver wants or needs.

So this presents an interesting problem, revolving solely around how the safety provisions are perceived, based upon the label they are given.

The advance in safety by using the arrester bed system is significant but perception of them suffers because of the negative connotations of the word *arrester* versus the positive connotations of the word *safety*, despite the result being identical.

Framing is important. It doesn't need to be complex but does make a difference.

JUST THE FACTS MA'AM

How a situation is described by witnesses can drastically affect an emergency response. Emergency call operators are not trying to waste precious time when they carefully gather details from anyone who calls an emergency telephone number. It's just that emergency services can be most effective if they have a clear understanding of what the emergency actually is.

I have had first-hand experience with this. When I was in my first year as a firefighter, I was temporarily posted to a fire station on the outskirts of the city. It was basically where the suburbs started to dwindle and the remaining properties could be considered more rural than urban.

One Saturday night we received a call at about eleven pm for us to assist paramedics with a suspected stroke victim. Usually, firefighters are called upon for medical assistance in circumstances like this simply to provide a bit of muscle and help lift victims off the ground and onto a stretcher, especially if the victim is of large proportions.

En route to this particular emergency we were contacted by our communications centre and advised of the situation. Apparently the relatives of the suspected stroke victim were still on the phone to the ambulance service and were describing to them what the circumstances were. This in turn was being relayed bit by bit to the Fire Service Communication Centre and eventually, to us.

Allegedly, a party was in progress at the property that we were heading to and one of the attendees had collapsed in the toilet and was only semiconscious.

Shortly thereafter we received further information that the ambulance had arrived and confirmed that an older gentleman had indeed collapsed in an outdoor toilet and was trapped inside. Because the door was locked, we would probably be required to force entry into the toilet to free the victim.

Not long after this message we arrived at the property in question. A few guests were still on the footpath next to the ambulance and signalled to us that we were in the right location. As we dismounted from the fire appliance the guests began telling us what had happened and offered to escort us to the scene of the problem.

Because it was dark with only one distant street light in view we stopped to grab some lighting equipment as well as hand held torches. We already knew that we'd probably be required to break down a door or at the least take it off its hinges, so each of us grabbed various tools and pieces of equipment to take with us. This delay whilst we equipped ourselves nearly always agitates people that are involved with an emergency or accident and especially if it involves a relative or friend. As an emergency service worker you can never seem to move fast enough to satisfy people when an emergency is at hand.

Nonetheless, we headed off down the dark driveway armed with various pieces of equipment and escorted by friends and relatives. The music was still playing and as we rounded the side of the house we were greeted by approximately forty people still engaged in the party and about five other people plus two paramedics crouched around the outdoor toilet located to one side of the back yard.

As we approached the outhouse we could see and hear that the paramedics were attempting to talk to the victim through the door to gauge his condition. One of the distressed relatives kindly informed us that the outhouse's trapped occupant was 'Uncle Bill.' The voice coming softly through the toilet door was that of an older sounding male which confirmed that it was most likely Uncle Bill.

The paramedics were attempting to gauge his condition and after a few minutes of conversation through the locked door, it appeared that he had collapsed against the door after relieving himself and now could not move or feel his left arm - all the initial indicators of a heart attack or stroke. Rapid access to Uncle Bill was needed.

Not only was the outhouse door locked but Uncle Bill was lying against the other side of it so simply taking the sledgehammer to the door would do more harm than good. Fortunately, the hinges for the door had their hinge-pins located on the outside. We set to with a hammer and a centre-punch to knock the pins out of each of the three hinges.

We started with the lowest hinge and then the centre hinge. Because of Uncle Bill's weight against the base of the door it began to lean outward once we had removed the bottom and centre hinge. That allowed two of us to grab hold of the door from both sides and simply lever it outward and upward, ripping the top hinge from the wooden door.

The paramedics grabbed Uncle Bill as he rolled out of his confinement and began a rapid assessment of his condition. First they put an oxygen mask on him and began taking his vital signs. Uncle Bill was a little groggy and still insisted that he was unable to move his left arm. In preparation for his transport to hospital we firefighters arranged and prepared the patient gurney so that Uncle Bill could be placed upon it without delay.

It was at this point that we firefighters ran out of meaningful contributions to the situation and it became more of a paramedic issue so we tended to other seemingly trivial matters like additional lighting and clearing the path between our current location and the ambulance.

It was at this point that my Station Officer noticed and pointed out to the paramedics that the victim's left shirt sleeve cuff was buttoned to the fly on his trousers! Once unbuttoned, Uncle Bill miraculously regained the use of his arm and soon began complaining about the pins and needles as the blood began to return to it. He'd been lying on his left arm throughout this ordeal.

His slurred speech turned out to be the product of his blood alcohol content which, if I recall correctly, was well over the legal driving limit. This was also the sole reason behind Uncle Bill buttoning his sleeve to his fly and falling over.

Whilst the story ended well for Uncle Bill, who would perhaps suffer no more than a few bruises, a hangover and some embarrassment, the same could not be said for the outhouse which had come off second best after four firemen had wreaked havoc upon it.

Due to the circumstances that converged to make this an unusual and even funny story, the way the situation was 'framed' to both the fire brigade and the ambulance service shows why nearly everyone involved concluded upon the stroke or heart attack diagnosis.

Undoubtedly, the situation wouldn't have evolved the same if the victim wasn't trapped inside the outhouse or if the event had happened during daylight hours or a myriad of other variables that may have resulted in the situation being assessed and framed differently to those that responded.

Peter F. Drucker said in his book, The Effective Executive, about making effective decisions, that all decisions should start with the facts yet rarely are the facts presented actually facts, instead, they are merely opinions.

This is a trap for the inexperienced. To accept what one is told without question or assessing the situation yourself exposes you to falling prey to other people's assumptions and opinions.

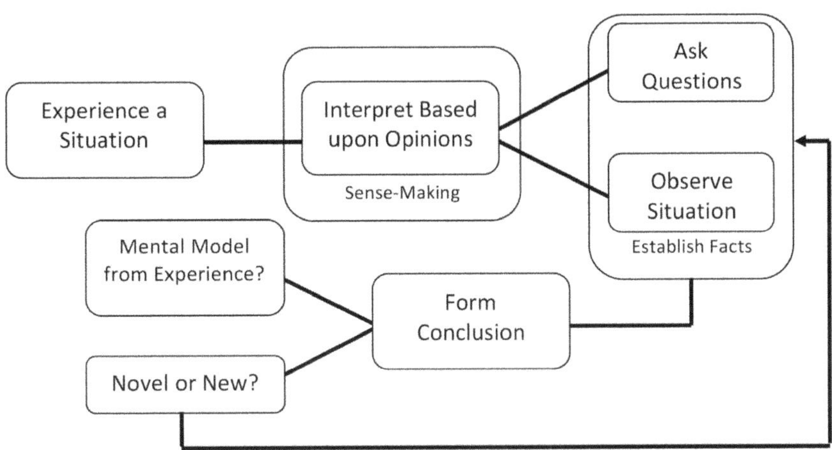

MINDSETS COME FROM EXPERIENCE

That is why the concept of 'mindsets' is controversial. Our mindsets have evolved from a lifetime of experience and frame the cues of the situation or problem that confronts us, so we can make sense of everything. The more experience we have, the more mental-models we have to draw upon.

In the model above we can see that if we encounter a situation that we are required to act upon, we may be at the mercy of acting on other people's accounts of the situation (opinions) or we may be relying upon our own sensory inputs to come to terms with the situation (sense-making). There are two ways forward here in that we can seek additional information from others or continue to experience the situation ourselves. Both of these activities allow us to establish what we conclude is the *actual* situation, which may differ from what we were originally told or thought. Once we have concluded our diagnosis of the situation we can evaluate our toolbox of mental models and compare to see if this situation is familiar or entirely new or novel.

If the situation is novel and something we have not experienced before, then more questions may be required to interpret the situation further before deciding upon a course of action.

There's a wise saying that I have adopted in the emergency world and use it in many of my training sessions and that is, "Good judgment comes from experience and experience comes from poor judgment."

Whilst you may agree with this sentiment, it unfortunately becomes the mantra of many people and businesses alike. They seek to prevent mistakes rather than seek new knowledge; expertise if you like.

We saw in Chapter 4 that heuristic decision making is essentially mental shortcuts involving known solutions that may not be perfect but they are good enough. Think about how you have arrived at some of the shortcuts and work-arounds that you use in your daily life and I'll bet they came to be in your repertoire because you once made a mistake.

I remember burning my fingers on a baking dish my mother had taken out of the oven when I was a child. Poor judgement? – Indeed. Experience gained? – You bet. Mental model developed about things that have been in the oven? – Stays with me to this day.

Before I proceed, I'm not advocating that anyone reading this book should entice their child to touch a hot dish straight out of the oven. There are many things we learn by being taught and there's just as much we learn from firsthand experience. It's this experience that's going to underpin our ability to arrive at decisions much faster but first, we must release our fear of making mistakes.

In Chapter 4 I wrote about the Pratfall Effect where our mistakes may even encourage people to empathise with us. That's certainly not to say we should go about our days actively trying to make mistakes, that's foolhardy. However, there is a difference between avoiding mistakes and seeking to improve, consequently developing expertise.

NOT GOOD ENOUGH?

One reason that prevents people from taking their best guess or going on instinct is that old chestnut – fear. "What if I'm wrong?" If the situation is such that others can be consulted, additional data can be examined and time is not against you, then all well and good. However, if a deadline looms large then you can feel like Johnny on the spot.

We are all our own worst critic and at the same time we'd all like to be perfect. That's a tall order and I'm sure that there is almost no one who really and truly believes that they are and have always been perfect. I've often said that the person who has never made a mistake has never made a decision.

The major decision making barrier for the majority of people is getting it wrong and everyone noticing or so you may think.

Enter, The Spotlight Effect. Basically, our mistakes are not noticed as much as we imagine they are. The self-doubt or even embarrassment that we feel each time we make a mistake does not truly reflect reality. People aren't really paying that much attention to our moments of failure anywhere near as much as we think they are. The perception that we are under constant scrutiny is simply in our minds.

One set of studies in 2000, by a team of psychologists at Cornell University, put it to the test and after taking the results into account gave the spotlight effect its name. To test their theory, psychologists asked participants to put on a shirt with a large picture of someone's face on the front and then walk into a room filled with students. After each participant left the room, they were asked to estimate how many of the students in the room would be able to remember whose face was on their T-shirt.

The observers in the room were also asked if they could remember whose face had been on the shirt of the person who had entered the room. The study was conducted under the guise of it being "a study on memory."

Participants who were asked to wear the shirt drastically overestimated how many people would remember Barry Manilow (a face each participant said that they were embarrassed to wear) as the face prominently emblazoned on their shirt. The estimations of the test subjects were twice as high as the actual number.

Even when their T-shirt had a face that wasn't embarrassing, the wearers still overestimated how many people would remember who was on their shirt.

Coming to grips with the reality that we are all under the spotlight less than we think we are should give us some comfort and confidence to make a decision, even if it isn't perfect. We make the best decision based upon the facts at hand in relation to our treasure chest of known solutions to recognised problems. Of course, as we've discussed in previous chapters, we continue to monitor, evaluate and adjust as we gain clarity from our actions.

FEAR OF BEING WRONG

Too many people struggle with this affliction daily. The cost is high. There is the anxiety we spoke of in the first chapter, the lost opportunities and of course decreasing morale in those around you and perhaps yourself.

As Sir Ken Robinson, author, speaker and international advisor on education said, *"If you're not prepared to be wrong, you'll never come up with anything original."*

For fear of being wrong, many people never participate actively in things or ask questions. This has a range of negative effects on learning and your opportunities to gain experience and consequently develop expertise.

In classroom environments, students learn not only from the teacher but from each other. That may be at school, university or even at work. If participants or students withdraw, the potential for a shared learning environment is removed.

One other paradox is that if students are often wrong but are too afraid to ask questions, then they don't learn the right answer or because students are often right but fear being wrong so much that they don't participate, they miss out on a possibly rewarding experience.

Fear of being wrong or being judged by our peers, limits our creativity. Playing it safe and erring on the side of conformity may reduce your chance of rejection or embarrassment but it will also reduce your chance of learning, growing and developing expertise.

Bill Gates, founder of Microsoft, puts it this way, *"Success is a lousy teacher. It seduces smart people into thinking they can't lose."*

BLAME IT ON RIO

One thing that can constantly undermine our decision making and enhance our fear of being wrong is blaming ourselves for our mistakes or what is sometimes worse, blaming others. One of the more popular concepts in psychology, the Fundamental Attribution Error is when people attribute the cause of an outcome to a person instead of a situation.

If the mistake is yours then own up to it, if only to yourself. In a classroom setting, the "wrong" answer is often more educational than the "right" answer. When I have conducted emergency response training I've had occasions where the wrong answer actually shed more light on the subject and helped participants understand the topic better than when the right answer was given.

Remember, learning has two definitions and it's both right *and* wrong. We use the same word, "learn," to describe a situation in which you receive new information and also a situation in which you update that information because your wrong answer bought it to your attention.

Acknowledging that everyone is wrong sometimes and nobody is right all the time is a step forward in removing any misgivings about being wrong. More often than not, we don't actually notice other people being wrong about something so, to us, it seems as though we are wrong more often than the people around us. (The Pratfall Effect) In reality, everybody is wrong occasionally.

As Dr. Seuss says, *"Those who matter don't mind and those who mind don't matter."*

A BLIP ON THE RADAR

One other thing that will help overcome the fear of being wrong is to stop treating being wrong like an abnormality. Consider this: Are you right more often than you are wrong? Every single day of your life there are things you get right. You remember to look for traffic before crossing the road, you remember your own birthday and if you're married you remember your wedding anniversary, don't you? (Hint: If you don't you'd better find out!)

The number and list of things you know is staggering. But *knowing* is just as often accompanied by *not knowing*. Comedian Steven Wright says he often asks this question of prospective employers when he attends job interviews, *"If you were driving along in a car at the speed of light and you turned on the headlights, could you now see where you were going?"* When the employer answers, *"I don't know."* Steven replies, *"Well, I don't want to work for you then."*

You see, we don't beat ourselves up for all the things we don't know (which is a lot, including driving cars at the speed of light), so why should we kick ourselves for being "wrong?" It's as natural as being "right."

THE SILENT MAJORITY

It's happened to all of us. More often than not, someone else is thinking the same thing. Have you ever had an answer to a question, remained silent, and then someone else gives the same answer you would have given? Whether the other person was right or wrong, the point is that you weren't alone in your thinking. You're simply not that different from the majority of those around you.

PROGRESS FROM BEING WRONG

The most intelligent people *try* to be wrong on purpose. They're called scientists. All of human advancement rests upon the principles of scientific investigation, which requires trial and error.

The best scientists try everything they can to prove themselves (and each other) wrong, because they want their results to be as accurate as possible. All of us benefit each time someone in scientific research is wrong. Prolific inventor Thomas Edison once said, *"I have not failed. I've just found ten thousand ways that won't work."*

If we develop the habit of looking at being wrong as being one step closer to being right then we break down the barriers to our hesitations about making a decision. Once you form a habit, it will become easier. Even if you aren't comfortable about speaking your mind or being wrong at first, with time it will become seem natural.

IN AN EMERGENCY

Theodore Roosevelt summed it up best when he said, *"In any moment of decision, the best thing you can do is the right thing, the next best thing you can do is the wrong thing and the worst thing you can do is nothing."*

Emergencies are dynamic and evolving situations. Indecision gets you nowhere and will not resolve the situation, so much so that many militaries around the world have a saying that, "Any decision, even the wrong decision, is better than no decision." As you can see, this is a simplified version of Teddy Roosevelt's statement above.

A WORD OF CAUTION

The notion that making any decision is advancing your understanding of the situation, needs to be matched with a level of sensibility.

Perhaps the saying should actually be revised to read any *sensible* decision, even a *well-considered yet* wrong decision, is better than no decision.

I have been challenged by participants in my decision making training courses that have taken the quote verbatim. I have even had questions such as, *"So if today is the day that I decide I can fly, should I jump off a cliff? After all, that's any decision!"*

Whilst I generally constrain myself from advising that person to do us all a favour and go and put that theory into practice, I mean that making a decision *in relation to the problem at hand* is the intent.

THINK – No one is right one hundred percent of the time.

DECIDE – Seek expertise and knowledge rather than simply try to avoid mistakes.

ACT – Practice doing things outside your comfort zone. Trust yourself and start believing that "putting yourself out there" really doesn't come with as many risks as you might have thought.

Chapter 6

IF IT LOOKS LIKE A DUCK …

"The human brain is an incredible pattern matching machine."

- Jeff Bezos

Chapter 6 -
IF IT LOOKS LIKE A DUCK ...

I have been accused many times of stereotyping and I am guessing that I am not alone here? You're probably thinking to yourself as you're reading this, *"Yep, me too. I've also fallen in that trap!"*

Well, here's some controversy. I'm not going to call it a trap per se. Simply put, nearly every stereotype is a stereotype because more often than not many preconceptions or commonly accepted norms are indeed, correct. Stereotypes can be about objects, situations or people. Yes, yes all right, I know that it's not socially acceptable to stereotype because you may indeed make assumptions that are entirely wrong and that stereotypes about people are almost taboo nowadays. However, you've got to start somewhere when sizing up a situation, assessing the circumstances or gathering the facts. It simply saves time and makes the process of gathering data simpler and less confusing if you have basic reference data to draw upon, whether that data is from your own experience or commonly accepted norms.

Yes, there are some pitfalls but we'll examine those shortly. For now, let's examine how stereotyping can actually help us.

Stereotypes can help make sense of the world. It's a way of categorising information that helps to simplify and classify information. Therefore, if we have our own personal mental library to draw upon when the need arises, we'll find that information is more easily identified, recalled, predicted and used.

Many social research experiments have supported the theory of how stereotypes function as time and energy savers that allow people to act more efficiently. Similarly, other studies suggest that stereotypes are people's biased perceptions of their social context. This is when people use stereotypes as shortcuts to make sense of their social environment, making a person's task of understanding their world less cognitively demanding.

So let's be realistic here. We all stereotype all the time, we probably just don't catch ourselves doing it. Think about it. The next time you walk into a pub and encounter a dozen Hells Angels bikers propping up the bar, do you automatically assume there's going to be trouble or that you've definitely walked into the wrong bar? And yet nothing may eventuate and you may even find yourself chatting with so-called rough bikers and being surprised that your initial assumptions were wrong. Then again, maybe not!

NOT ALL IS AS YOU IMAGINE

I recall the first time I encountered an acquaintance when I was much younger. I'll call him Graham, which is not his real name. Graham was about six foot three inches and heavy set. He commanded attention when he walked into a room. He had long dark hair and a beard as well as a few visible tattoos. Graham also rode a motorbike and as such, regularly wore 'biker' clothing such as leather jackets, denim and heavy boots. He looked rough and the sort of guy you wouldn't want to upset. Initially, I too avoided him because of my stereotype beliefs that if I dare say anything to such a humungous and rough looking dude, he'd probably squash me like a bug. That was until the day a mutual friend introduced us to one another.

Graham, despite his appearance, was soft-spoken and articulate. He had a couple of university degrees and his passion besides his motorbike was ….. Morris dancing.

Morris dancing is an English folk dance. Participants usually wear bell pads on their shins and wield a handkerchief between thumb and forefinger in each hand.

Graham was definitely not the stereotype I had imagined. I even had to suppress laughter when I pictured such an imposing individual engaged in Morris dancing. (Sorry Morris dancers, no offence intended).

Contrast my assumptions and introduction to Graham with another biker experience that I encountered when I was much younger.

OFTEN THINGS *ARE* AS THEY SEEM

I had just started recruit training with the fire service in my hometown of Adelaide. The girl I was dating at the time had a passion for a band called the 'Modes.' We had been to a variety of venues around town to watch and listen to them play. It was with dismay then, when watching them one Friday night, that they announced they would be disbanding after one final gig the following Saturday at the Exeter Hotel. There was no discussion required; my girlfriend and I couldn't miss their last performance ever.

Throughout the week I did my research and located the Exeter Hotel in Rundle Street in Adelaide's CBD.

Saturday night came and with girlfriend in tow, I strolled into the Exeter Hotel that was partly deserted and quiet as a library. Rather confused I asked the barman where the band was. He replied, *"No band here mate."* I assured him that the Modes were indeed advertising that tonight they were playing their final gig at the Exeter Hotel. Fortunately the one bar-fly propping up the bar a short distance from where I stood offered the suggestion, *"You probably mean the Exeter Hotel at Port Adelaide."*

Into the car we hopped and off to Port Adelaide we drove to a hotel I'd never been to before. Fortunately we found it in good time and as I parked the car we could hear the familiar tunes of the Modes starting their final performance. We rushed inside.

Now, this was the 1980s. Consequently, I was wearing skin tight light coloured stretch denims with high top white 'Reebok pumps,' a white shirt and had blonde hair. I mention this because as we rushed into the venue it very quickly became apparent that this was a biker pub. White was not the choice colour of dress.

I sized up the situation quite quickly and (yes, I stereotyped) concluded that we didn't fit in with this crowd to say the least. Hastily we made a beeline for a table in a booth in the corner of the room, from where we hopefully wouldn't attract the attention of the much older, black leather clad crowd.

After a couple of songs, my girlfriend prompted me to go and get us a couple of drinks. Nervously I left the safety of the booth and headed to the bar. I think the barman took pity on me and asked me what I wanted quite quickly. Because the music was so loud I had to basically shout my order to him at the top of my voice. To make my order even more audible I stood on the bar's foot-rail and lifted myself up and leaned partway over the bar. As loud as I could, I shouted, *"I'll have a beer and ... "* just as the song that the Modes were playing had a two second silent break in the song. I use the term silent break in which a song regularly uses a pause in the music, to silent yet dramatic effect. Unless of course that silence is filled by that young blonde guy in a white shirt standing on the bar rail yelling at the top of his voice *"... a Fluffy Duck!"*

Well this incurred the derision of most bar patrons and I'm confident to this day that it was the catalyst of a bar fight that happened after some patrons saw fit to jostle me and some others shouted to leave the guy (me) alone. Nonetheless, we used the ensuing fight as cover to flee the venue.

So, the latter experience reinforced to me that my initial assumptions regarding the hotel's clientele were exactly as I had envisaged. My stereotype for that social setting dictated to me that trouble was awaiting an opportunity to erupt and I was right. Yet that same stereotype led me to make incorrect judgements when I first encountered Graham and subsequently learning of his Morris dancing passion.

STEREOTYPING GETS YOU TO THE START LINE FASTER

Stereotyping is what gives a police officer their street-smarts or the fire officer their 'intuition' when it comes to arriving at a situation and coming to grips quickly with the state-of-play. Police officers do look at three people lurking in an alley and stereotype this gathering of more than one person in a dark lane as a drug deal or mugging or any other scenario that has come to represent a typical occurrence that would conform to this context.

This is where street-smart comes into play. Knowing there is a soup kitchen offering food to the homeless nearby may mean that the initial assumption is three homeless folk enjoying a meal together. Knowing that prostitutes frequent the area to ply their trade leads to another conclusion and the same goes for drug dealers. Stereotyping will differ in all of us and from location to location, dependent upon what events and people are commonplace.

The upside of this behaviour is that it saves emergency service personnel from having to start from scratch every time they encounter any sort of emergency. It is easier to approach a situation and discount preconceived assumptions (stereotype) than approach a possibly dangerous situation with a completely empty mind and discover and learn as you go each and every time.

This is not to say that stereotyping is always accurate or correct. An incorrect assumption acted upon is where the concept of stereotyping cops a bad rap.

ACTIONS AND WORDS

It can be beneficial to approach a situation with your own preconceived assumptions in mind and then discount what turns out to be misleading or wrong. Stereotyping's bedfellows are prejudice, bias and discrimination.

Stereotypes are generally regarded as what you think about a situation, person or people or object and yet may occur without you actually realising it. Prejudice or bias is the outcome of stereotyping and discrimination is one of the behavioural components or actions as the result of prejudice. In short, prejudice is the emotional response and discrimination refers to the actions arising from it.

Many of us are likely familiar with any number of wrongful arrest lawsuits that alleges racial profiling or civil lawsuits that arise from someone being hired for a job in preference to another applicant, whether that's due to their gender, religion or sexual orientation and so on. Don't get me wrong, stereotyping can be detrimental, unfair, unjust and in some cases downright evil.

To borrow a couple of popular analogies when describing the good and the bad of stereotyping, you could write a book about how stereotyping is detrimental but you could fill a library with where it's helpful.

And - if it looks like a duck, quacks like a duck and walks like a duck… it's a duck!

Used with an objective approach and a willingness to admit being wrong, stereotyping gives emergency service personnel a head start on defining the context of the emergency they are facing.

PUTTING YOUR STEREOTYPES TO WORK

What impact does it have in the workplace? Generally, when the issue of stereotyping arises, it is always in a negative manner and people are chastised for it. Most articles in magazines and online about this topic speak of stereotyping as a corporate evil that must be stamped out at all costs. Few mention that the negative side of stereotyping is acting upon one's bias or prejudice arising from a stereotype.

Here are a few examples that I found online in no time at all.

Example 1. A manager doesn't ask an older employee to learn a new computer program because she thinks he won't be able to learn it. "Older people are frightened of new technology."

Is it wrong to stereotype older employees or people in this way? No, because many of us have indeed spent plenty of time on the phone with a parent or older person trying to explain to them the simplest of computer or smartphone functions and it is a fact that many people over the age of sixty haven't had a lifetime of computer or technical gadgets to learn from. Again, that's not in any way to say all older people are technically challenged.

What is actually wrong is acting on that stereotype and as the example says, not asking the employee to learn a new computer program.

Example 2. An employee with a new male manager doesn't go to him with a problem because she thinks he won't be a good listener. "Men don't communicate as well as women."

First and foremost, I'm not sure this stereotype is quite correct. I think it might be slightly more accurate if it were, "Men don't communicate like women." Nonetheless, stereotyping men as having different communication skills or styles to women is nothing new. However, as with the example before, acting upon this preconceived prejudice without asking the new male manager if he is receptive to help with a problem, is a problem.

Whilst the two examples are only the tip of the iceberg and both are using the workplace as an example, the same scenarios play out in sporting teams, schools, universities and many other social settings.

USE THE FORCE, LUKE

So as you can see, stereotypes can be misleading and can be inaccurate, untrue and completely wrong. However, emergency management practitioners use them all the time to turbo boost their ability to interpret a situation or set the context.

Acting upon those stereotypes without further consideration or investigation is foolhardy and can lead to the dark side of stereotyping upon which most assumptions about this human habit are based.

Used wisely and sensibly, there is no harm in getting to the start line in record time with stereotyping.

HOW TO GUARD AGAINST STEREOTYPES

The next time you have an interaction with someone, take ten seconds to objectively judge whether you have used stereotypes to fill in the blanks or whether you really know the person.

By pausing and reflecting to see if you have actually listened to their point of view means that you're on track to avoid the stereotype 'trap' I mentioned earlier.

Keep an open mind and prepare to be surprised. You might find you have more stereotypes about others than you realised. Ask open-ended questions to draw out their thoughts, ideas or opinion.

Lose your fear of being wrong. In this instance you've approached a situation or person with a preconceived notion and no one but you will know you had a misleading impression beforehand unless, of course, you made your assumptions known – always a risky move.

THINK - We all have stereotypes embedded in our mind that we use to ease our decision making load on a daily basis, whether we realise it or not.

DECIDE - Using stereotypes to kick start our understanding of a situation, event, people, person or object is beneficial and used in a fair and sensible manner is not necessarily negative and will speed up your decision making.

ACT – Ask questions and actively try to disprove your initial stereotype. This will ensure that whilst you may have judged the situation correctly from the outset, you are prepared to be wrong and change your opinion and actions on this occasion.

Chapter 7

NATURALISTIC DECISION MAKING

"I think it's very important to have a feedback loop where you're constantly thinking about what you've done and how you could be doing it better."

- Elon Musk

Chapter 7
NATURALISTIC DECISION MAKING

Our whole lives are stored and categorised in our memory. Well almost. If I asked you to recall exactly what you had for breakfast last year on November the third, do you think you could recall it? Unless you religiously eat exactly the same meals for every single breakfast every single day without fail you'd probably struggle to recall details such as these.

Our memory would be an extremely crowded place if we actually did remember *everything.*

So for most of us, we commit to memory, experiences that stand out in some way. Experiences that taught us something, for example, when you first learnt to ride a bike or drive a car. Experiences that caused an emotional response such as the death of a loved one or the funniest movie or stage show you've seen, getting married or even the birth of your child. I mentioned in the chapter on heuristics that burning my hand by touching a dish straight out of the oven was something that I definitely remember.

All of these are milestones in our lives and feature prominently in our memories for reasons that are important to us. So, how is it that we can remember falling off a bicycle when we were five years old but can't remember if we had a cup of coffee at breakfast last Wednesday?

TWO SPEED THINKING

Daniel Kahneman is a psychologist most noted for his work in the psychology of judgment and decision making, as well as behavioural economics. He is currently a senior scholar and faculty member emeritus at Princeton University's Department of Psychology. In 2002, Kahneman received the Nobel Memorial Prize in Economic Sciences, despite being a research psychologist.

In his 2012 book, Thinking Fast and Slow, Kahneman contends that there are two modes of thought and decision making that we all possess. He called these two ways of thought, System One and System Two.

System One is fast with seemingly automatic responses or actions. It occurs with each of us when we do frequent tasks or perform routine actions such as walking, eating and drinking, breathing and standing up or sitting down. We rarely have to think these things through, we just do them. You could consider them subconscious.

System One also encompasses things that are more complex and less biological than breathing. For most adults, the question, "What does two plus two equal?" probably results in the recipient answering "Four," before you can even finish the last word of the sentence.

What's going on in our brain is that we don't have to do mental arithmetic to work that calculation out. We just know and because we 'just know,' we find that the answer comes very quickly.

It's because we can do so much without really having to concentrate (System One thinking) that we can drink a cup of coffee and enjoy it at the time, yet not really recall the experience some days, weeks or months later.

How many times have you driven home in your car after work and whilst driving, you've been reflecting on your day or you've enjoyed the music on the radio or the chit-chat of the radio announcer and then, all of a sudden, you're home in your driveway. And you can't really recall the drive home even though it's something that you've just been doing for the last thirty minutes or so.

That's because your System One thinking has been making all the decisions about traffic, traffic lights, lane changes, speed and braking. You have done it so often that you don't actually have to consciously 'think' about your actions.

Because so much of our lives is familiar to us, System One thinking can easily cope. There's little or no learning taking place because all is as it seems and nothing is unfamiliar. Therefore, there's no need to commit it to memory.

System Two thinking is much more labour intensive. It's slow, effortful, logical, calculating and conscious thought. For most of us, it is something we don't do nearly as much or as frequently as System One thinking. Therefore, our brain considers it hard work. So hard in fact, that we often stop doing other, even subconscious things so that we can devote our energy to System Two thinking.

For example, have you ever been trying to concentrate on reading instructions for your new DVR or IKEA furniture that you've just bought and the kids have loud music playing? Did you find yourself telling the kids to turn the music down because you're trying to think? Perhaps you've told someone to stop talking you whilst you were trying to recall someone's phone number?

This System Two thinking requires us to stop and think. It's what we draw upon when we encounter something new or novel. Consequently, it is why we find it hard to come up with a brilliant idea when the pressure is on.

It's also why many people find themselves 'stuck' looking for a decision when they encounter a situation that they are unfamiliar with. System Two thinking *is* hard and emergency situations don't lend themselves to creativity easily. Many people find that when thought doesn't come easily, no thoughts come at all.

Time is a critical factor affecting decision making. Time pressure creates stress and stress hampers our ability for System Two thinking.

THE OODA LOOP

Colonel John Boyd graduated from the University of Iowa and served as a US Air Force officer from July 8th, 1951, until his retirement on August 31st, 1975. During the time that he was a pilot, Boyd flew F-86 Sabres during the Korean War.

Boyd was later assigned to the USAF Weapons School, primarily based at Nellis Air Force Base in Nevada, USA and became head of the Academic Section, writing the tactics manual for the school.

During this time, Colonel Boyd, after analysing the success of the American F-86 fighter plane compared with that of the Soviet MIG-15, developed a decision making model for pilots in air-to-air combat.

Boyd contended that although the MIG was faster and could turn better, the American plane won more battles because the pilot's field of vision was far superior.

This improved field of vision gave the pilot a clear competitive advantage. The pilot could assess the situation better and faster than an opponent and could out-manoeuvre the enemy pilot, who would be caught off-guard, wouldn't know what to expect and would start making mistakes.

Boyd's key concept was that the decision cycle process by which an entity reacts to an event is the key to victory. In essence, his theory was that, despite technical or positional disadvantage, to be able to create situations wherein one can make appropriate decisions more quickly than one's opponent results in success.

Boyd called his decision making model, the OODA Loop.

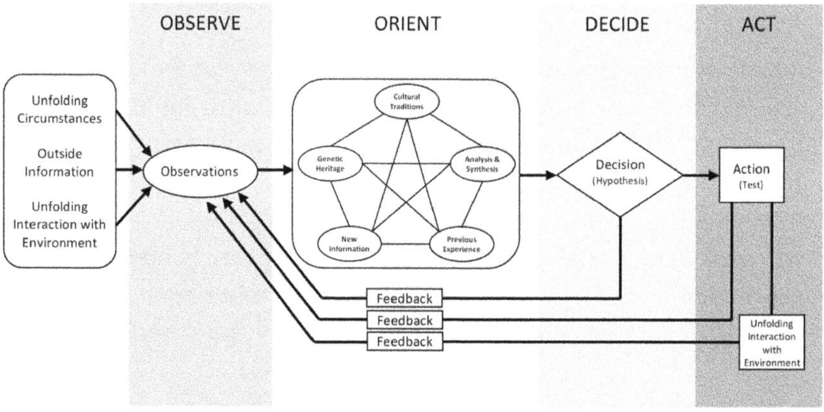

Harry Hillaker, chief designer of the General Dynamics F-16 fighter jet said of the OODA theory, "*Time is the dominant parameter. The pilot who goes through the OODA cycle in the shortest time prevails because their opponent is caught responding to situations that have already changed.*"

This all may sound rather academic and methodical but you probably already do this without thinking about it. It's just that Boyd managed to design a model and give it a name. You're probably more familiar with terms like thinking 'on the fly' or thinking 'on your feet' or even flying 'by the seat of your pants.' Basically, it means that you are changing your decisions and actions in relation to the changing circumstances around you. Let's be honest, if constantly changing your decisions and actions works for fighter pilots, then it's certainly going to be of benefit to you.

Contrasting Kahneman's System One and Two thinking, the OODA Loop seeks to tap into System One (quick thinking) by acknowledging the pilot's existing skills and knowledge about air combat and quickly matching them to the unfolding situation that the pilot is experiencing.

Understanding the 'Loop'

Called the OODA Loop, the model outlines a four-point decision loop that supports quick, effective and proactive decision making. It is described as a loop because there is no actual beginning or end due to the constant requirement to evaluate and re-evaluate and adjust your actions to match the changing dynamics.

The four stages are:

OBSERVE – Collect current information from as many sources as practically possible.

ORIENT – Analyse this information and use it to update your current reality.

DECIDE – Determine a course of action.

ACT – Follow through on your decision.

You cycle through the OODA Loop by observing the results of your actions, assessing whether you've achieved the results you intended, reviewing and revising your initial decision and moving to your next action.

It wasn't long after Boyd developed his model that its potential applications in business soon became apparent. Success in business generally comes from being a step ahead of your competitors whilst also being able to react to trends in your particular market.

RECOGNITION PRIMED DECISION MAKING

In addition to the OODA Loop, military, law enforcement and emergency service personnel make heavy use of a decision system called Naturalistic Decision Making (NDM) or Recognition Primed Decision Making (RPDM).

Some of the first funding into decision making research came from the US Army and Navy in the mid-1980s. The US Navy became interested in naturalistic decisions following an incident in 1988 when US Navy Aegis cruiser USS Vincennes shot down an Iranian commercial airliner, mistaking it for a hostile attacker.

Of course, this was a serious international incident causing many lives to be lost. Naturally, the navy needed to investigate and fully understand how an innocent commercial airliner was mistaken for a fighter jet and what were the decision processes leading up to the incident that allowed such a mistake to happen.

This incident happened shortly after other naval incidents that caused a loss of lives and prompted the US Navy in 1990, to initiate a project they termed TADMUS (Tactical Decision Making Under Stress). The project ran for approximately ten years.

One of the major findings that resulted from this study was the recognition that when a range of influencing factors converge, the stress they produce in the individual charged with making decisions can be enormous.

ENTER THE EMERGENCY SERVICES

One way of studying time critical situations that contain high stake decisions is to look at other professions that operate under similar circumstances.

One of the most prominent researchers in decision making under time pressure is Dr Gary Klein. In 1985, Klein developed what he termed a 'Recognition-Primed Decision' (RPD) model to describe how people actually make decisions in natural settings. His research was subsequently incorporated into US Army doctrine for command and control.

Klein studied all manner of emergency service and military personnel to understand what decision processes were actually used under the extreme circumstances that paramedics, doctors, pilots, firefighters, police and military commanders find themselves facing.

Klein described the influencing factors that a leader must make decisions under as:

- Ill-defined goals and ill-structured tasks
- Uncertainty, ambiguity and missing data
- Shifting and competing goals

- Dynamic and continually changing conditions
- Action feedback loops (real-time reactions to changed conditions)
- Time stress
- High stakes
- Multiple players (team factors)
- Organisational goals and norms

I'm quite sure that all of us have found ourselves in a situation that has one or more of these impediments to clear, rational thought and decision making. But how would you feel if you faced all of the above and a decision on what to do was up to you?

Klein focussed much of his attention on firefighters to research how they arrive at decisions so quickly. He eventually discovered that eighty percent of the decisions made on a fireground by the commander were made in less than a minute. That's quite a fertile environment for someone wanting to study decision making.

His initial interviews with fire commanders became a source of frustration for him because commander after commander insisted that they didn't make any decisions when on the fireground. They just 'did what they did.'

It quickly became clear that the traditional method for problem solving and decision making were of little use in a time pressure circumstance and that the fire commanders he was interviewing were relying upon a very different way of thinking.

ESP

It was after one fire commander informed Klein that he didn't know how he made fireground decisions and that perhaps it was ESP (Extra Sensory Perception) that Klein began to theorise that the commanders had developed such expertise at what they did that they could recognise situations within the situations that they encountered. Upon recognising something that they saw as familiar they mentally matched it with a known remedy. They were pattern-matching.

GOOD JUDGEMENT COMES FROM EXPERIENCE AND EXPERIENCE COMES FROM POOR JUDGEMENT

What is commonly accepted as the foundation for rapid decision making under the constraints mentioned previously is that heavy reliance is made on expertise. Expertise derived not only from training but more so from experience.

Experts in their field can make rapid decisions because of their ability to recognise cues in even the most unusual circumstances. The doctor in an emergency ward can use their expertise for rapid diagnosis of a patient. The police officer can identify if a suspect is lying or not and of course the firefighter can size up a fire and determine the most appropriate method of attack.

That is to say that each leader assesses the situation and judges if it is familiar or not. They do not focus on comparing different options.

Then courses of action are quickly evaluated by imagining how they will be carried out. They do not stop and conduct formal analysis and comparisons. (System Two thinking.)

Decision makers will usually look for the first workable option they can find, not the best option (heuristics and/or satisficing). Since the first option they consider is usually workable, they do not have to generate a large set of options to be sure they get a good one (remove and simplify).

Then they generate and evaluate options one at a time and do not bother comparing the advantages and disadvantages of alternatives. By imagining the option being carried out, they can spot weaknesses and devise ways to avoid these, thereby making the chosen option better.

The chosen course (the decision) is then put into action and is constantly evaluated and adjusted as necessary (OODA Loop).

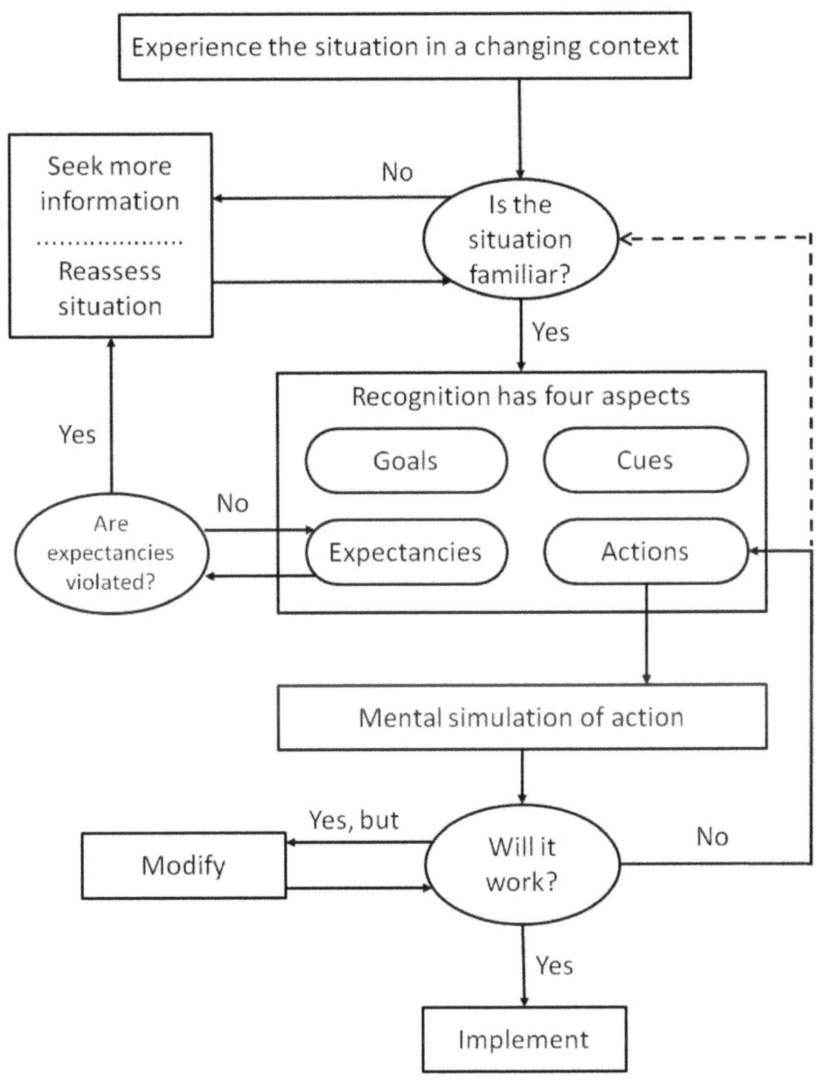
Experience the situation in a changing context
Seek more information
Reassess situation
No
Is the situation familiar?
Yes
Recognition has four aspects
Goals
Cues
Expectancies
Actions
Yes
No
Are expectancies violated?
Mental simulation of action
Yes, but
Modify
Will it work?
No
Yes
Implement

THINK – Even if a situation or problem is entirely new to us we may be able to recognise aspects of it that are familiar. (Pattern Matching, System One thinking)

DECIDE – Generate options and mentally evaluate if they'll work. (Satisfice)

ACT – If time is against you, implement the first workable option you generate and then evaluate and adjust as required. (OODA Loop and RPD)

Chapter 8

DILLY-DALLY AND DEADLINES

"Deadlines refine the mind. They remove variables like exotic materials and processes that take too long. The closer the deadline, the more likely you'll start thinking waaay outside the box."

– Adam Savage

Chapter 8
- DILLY-DALLY AND DEADLINES

Facing novel, one-off decisions where the outcome can't be accurately predicted is when procrastination reigns supreme.

In a workplace environment, leadership teams can agonise over decisions in situations like this, gathering more data, weighing options and seeking opinions. The result is an unprofitable delay in moving the organisation forward. The utopia that the team seeks but is actually 'waiting' for is that a clear answer or obvious choice emerges.

These types of decisions where there is no clear, right answer may delay an organisation for weeks, months or even years.

It's not just businesses that struggle with indecision hoping that the correct answer will arrive if delayed enough. We all know people who make decisions, like choosing a car or a house to buy, from a range of options and they make those decisions quite quickly. Then there are other people who spend ages agonising over the right colour lipstick or what to order at a restaurant or even which restaurant to eat at in the first place.

Generally speaking, most indecisive people are rational, intelligent adults who function perfectly well in their daily lives and suffer no problem with their duties and responsibilities. Yet, it seems that they cannot do much about their tendency to dither.

Many scientific studies indicate that the risk-reward system of the brain is closely related to the decision making process. It also appears that genetic variations in the genes related to the production of dopamine (the feel-good neurotransmitter) can make a person more or less indecisive than other people. These genes may raise or lower the perception of risk or reward when deciding upon a particular course of action and therefore may make a person reach a decision quickly or hesitate before making one.

So you can breathe a sigh of relief if you do find yourself constantly anguishing over even the simplest decisions as it may be your genetics that's to blame.

Another major component (and prime suspect in indecision) of our brains is the hippocampus. We all have two hippocampi, one on each side of our brain. It plays an important part in the consolidation of information from short-term memory to long-term memory and spatial navigation. Think of it if you will, as our brain's filing cabinet for our experiences, facts and details.

This part of the brain also assigns values to memories.

So the speed at which we can make a decision relies upon how quickly we can retrieve the memories from the hippocampus allowing us to put a value upon the choices we face. This is why it's always easy and quick when deciding to do something you like and how quickly you decide not to do something you don't like. Each memory has a value that is at either end of you value 'scale' and it doesn't take much effort to decide either way.

Where things get more difficult for us is when the choices we face are extremely similar or completely unfamiliar. They are in the middle region of our 'value scale' or not on it at all.

For example, think of a time when you were faced with two equally enticing and delicious meals on the menu at a restaurant or perhaps, where a restaurant menu doesn't contain any meals you are familiar with or contains ingredients that you have never tried before.

What's happening inside your brain when you recognise the menu items is that your brain's limbic system, including the hippocampus, is retrieving the memories of eating certain dishes last time you ate them and evaluating how much you enjoyed them. Your brain places a value on each of these choices and depending upon the choices you are faced with, may select a clear winner or may encounter two or three equal winners.

This, of course, dictates how quickly we can arrive at a decision. If there is one clear winner, the decision is a 'no-brainer' and we make our decision. If there are multiple equally attractive options, then the decision needs to be weighed and consequently we arrive at a decision more slowly.

Similarly, if we are entirely unfamiliar with the menu items and ingredients then we have little or no data filed in our hippocampus upon which to draw upon. Our decision then is going to be much less forthcoming.

If time is not of the essence and choices can be evaluated and discussed you may still find yourself stuck with two equally attractive choices which don't seem to present any clear winner.

ALL THINGS BEING EQUAL ... ALMOST

Choosing between two equally attractive alternatives is difficult. Even more so if there are *three* equally attractive alternatives. We are spoiled for choice nowadays and we constantly find ourselves weighing up alternatives with almost everything we do.

However, sometimes we do find ourselves at a junction where the features and benefits we have to choose from all seem equal. Perhaps it's as simple as the restaurant menu we spoke of previously or something a little more complex such as choosing a new computer or smartphone, deciding upon a course of action for your business such as a product launch or investment or perhaps which school to send your child to. How do we move the ball forward from this sticking point when the options all seem equally as good?

I often encounter this common sticking point with my clients in their emergency planning and preparedness. When it comes to the time, effort and cost of emergency training for their staff, I am often asked about the value of conducting emergency training. This is largely because the facility in question may be relatively new with state-of-the-art fire protection and security systems, so spending additional money, time and resources on something that may never happen seems like throwing money down the drain.

So my client is at a sticking point in their decision making. Should they spend time, energy and money on something perceived as unlikely to happen, yet be prepared and able to respond if it does? Or, should they avoid spending the time, energy and money on something perceived as unlikely to happen and devote those resources to the aim of the organisation and thus increase productivity and profit?

Let's explore my example above. If an organisation decides to prepare for an emergency and they encounter and respond effectively to that emergency, then it was the right decision, well done.

If an organisation decides not to prepare for an emergency and they never experience an emergency then it was the right decision, well done. Both were good decisions under those circumstances. However, exploring the downside paints a very different picture. If the organisation invests in emergency preparedness, planning and training and does not ever encounter an emergency, what are the downsides?

The cost of the planning and training, not only in actual monetary terms but also in that of lost employee time whilst attending training or exercises, is usually the first thing that comes to mind. Perhaps enthusiasm may also dwindle because people perceive that they are planning and training for something that has never happened.

If the organisation doesn't invest in emergency preparedness, planning and training and does encounter an emergency, what are the downsides? Looking at worst case scenario outcomes may include injury or death of the building's occupants, damage or destruction of the organisation's equipment, production line machinery or offices required to continue business or even total loss of the building itself. If there were injuries or fatalities then there will certainly be a coronial inquest and there may be reputation issues around the organisation's employee safety practices. Loss of the building and the other pressures listed above may lead to the organisation going out of business and consequently staff being laid off. I know that in this example I'm painting dire circumstances and I know that emergencies come in all shapes and sizes and may not cause any or all of the situations above but we're examining the *downside* of equally attractive decisions, so it pays to think worst case scenario.

This example put into a decision matrix looks like this. I've used a smiley face for where the right decision was perceived to have been made. For example, no time or money was spent on emergency training and no emergency has ever occurred. ☺

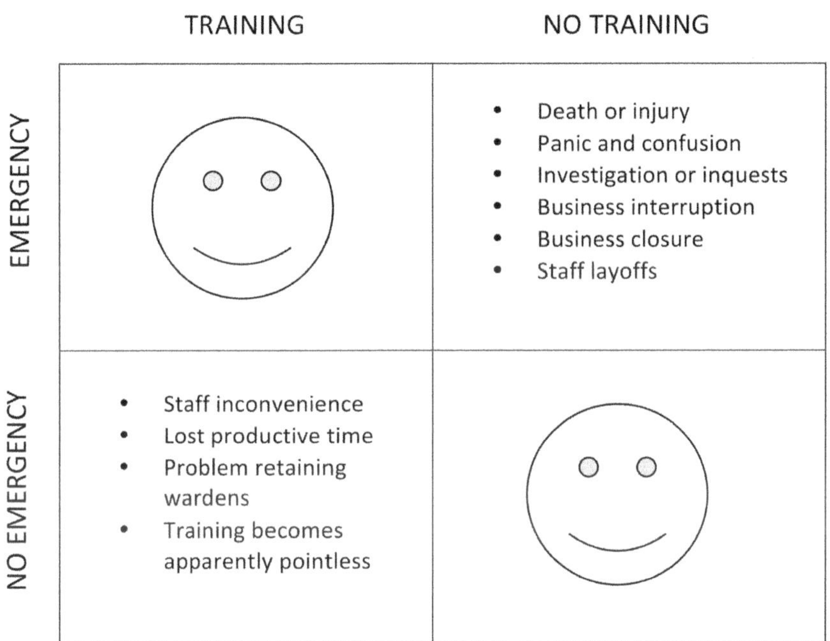

Considering *all* aspects of your options may make deciding between alternatives much more apparent. Rather than anguishing over which equally attractive option you like best, sometimes consider which equally attractive option will hurt you the least.

You certainly don't have to draw up a decision matrix like that above. With some decisions you can weigh the negative aspects quickly and simply in your head while others will take more time or require discussion. That's when a diagram like that above may prove useful.

Of course, in emergency situations you won't see firefighters or police officers stopping to draw decision matrices on a pocket notebook. There's too much to do and simply not enough time.

WHEN TIME IS NOT ON YOUR SIDE

So, our ability to store and retrieve our experiences and weigh them against the current circumstances or choices facing us will affect how quickly we can decide. However, to step it up a notch let's look at making those decisions but with a time constraint - a deadline.

This is the type of scenario that emergency service professionals face every day - ambiguous situations with tight time frames and rapidly evolving circumstances with no clear or right answer. Experience and the ability to put into play a 'best guess' is often the only choice. The doctor assessing the victim of a car accident prior to commencing treatment, the police officer having to draw and perhaps use their firearm, the fire officer determining whether to send firefighters into a burning house or fight the fire from outside.

There is no clear answer other than the deadline to make a decision before it's too late. We've just seen how decision making can be a time consuming process and time is an important resource for making optimal decisions. The allocation of less time than required or perceived as required for making a decision may cause a sense of time stress which may affect the quality of our decision processes.

Many situations such as a school or university exam or buy and sell decisions on the stock market and especially in emergency situations, shortage of time or a looming deadline is a normal characteristic of decision making.

People can react differently to time pressure. Some people rise to the challenge of a deadline and it focuses their attention on the problem at hand. Others find that the restriction of time to arrive at a decision inhibits their ability to have clear thoughts and they end up doing much worse than they would under normal conditions.

Some of the common failings that researchers have uncovered when looking at how test subjects respond to the demands of time constraints include:

- Reduced information search and processing
- Reduced range of alternatives and dimensions being considered
- An increased importance given to negative information
- Defensive reactions, such as neglect or denial of important information
- Adherence to the chosen alternative
- An increased tendency to filter and prioritise information; that is, information that is perceived as most important is processed first and then processing is continued until the deadline
- Forgetting important data
- Judgment and evaluation is impaired leading to wrong decisions

As you can see, the difficulty many of us face when dealing with complex or novel decisions is commonplace. When we struggle to think and search for an answer the addition of a deadline not only speeds us up and perhaps causes us to rise to the challenge but it often causes us to shortcut our way to the finish line. One potential reason is information processing overload caused by the need to process large amounts of information in short periods of time.

IT'S NOT ALL BAD NEWS THOUGH

This is where managers and leaders can move their organisation forward or we can personally motivate ourselves into action. Nothing motivates us more than a deadline.

If you find yourself anguishing over a decision or delaying getting started then mentally setting your own deadline can be the catalyst to action. If you are in a group setting and the issues on the table have been reasonably diagnosed, the choices are mutually attractive and yet no clear answer is obvious, set a deadline for a decision and decide. Just make the decision and move forward.

We discussed in previous chapters that fear of being wrong often holds people back from decisiveness. In the previous chapter we looked at John Boyd's OODA Loop and how his system was in fact, a loop. There's no real beginning or end just decisions, evaluations and corrections and so on.

In a sense, this fits neatly into what Peter Drucker described as, 'What gets measured gets done.' That is, if we have eternity to make a decision, that's more than likely how long it will take.

THINK – When the upside of your choices seem equally attractive then it may be prudent to look at the downsides as the measure of making a better decision.

DECIDE – Deadlines can prove detrimental yet when applied astutely, they can be the motivation to arrive at a timely decision.

ACT – Don't use your genes as an excuse for indecisiveness or procrastination. Acknowledge your indecisiveness, set yourself a deadline, make a decision and adjust if required.

Chapter 9

LEADERSHIP

"One of the tests of leadership is the ability to recognise a problem before it becomes an emergency."

- Arnold Glasgow

Chapter 9 - LEADERSHIP

Understanding how we as humans react to stress and our psychological predisposition to decision making under those circumstances is vital. This means that you can face up to the challenges of a crisis or those decisions you face every day with more confidence, more clarity and some 'tricks up your sleeve' that will stand you in good stead.

One of the interesting things that may result from improving your decision making abilities is that you enhance your leadership skills. Whether you aspire to be a recognised leader (manager) or not, it is becoming increasingly clear that leadership is in high demand in all walks of life.

I mentioned at the start of this book that the World Economic Forum released a report entitled "The Future of Jobs" in which over three hundred and fifty employers in nine different industries across fifteen of the world's leading economies were surveyed. The results of which were used to predict how technological advancements would challenge labour markets to evolve and how employers and employees will need to evolve to adapt to the workplace of 2020 and beyond.

Depending upon whom you choose to listen to or which research you believe, its forecast that up to a third of jobs today won't exist by 2020. It's not that jobs will just evaporate but the roles themselves will change.

The rapid rate of change in the workplace means that employers will be seeking employees with a different range of skills than those they look for today.

It comes as no surprise that 'people management' still ranked in the top ten highly desirable skills expected of an employee in 2020.

Studies of leadership consistently conclude that those we think of as leaders, not just managers, share common traits. That doesn't mean they all act alike or have the same training or even approach situations in an identical fashion but each will bring their individual approach when deciding and acting on any challenge that presents itself. That is usually the birthplace of those we label as leaders; their ability to rise to a challenge and to find meaning in, and even learn from, negative events. The skills required to triumph over adversity and emerge stronger and more committed are the same traits that make for exceptional leaders. Not a bad side-effect to effective decision making.

Decision making is an integral part of running a business, coaching a sports team and even managing the family budget but the question still remains, 'How are *good* decisions made?'

THE LONELIEST NUMBER IS ONE

Part of the answer is for you, the decision maker, to actively seek appropriate and accurate information and use your experience in interpreting that information. No matter whether the setting is corporate, social or family, consultation with and drawing upon the expertise of others also helps, as does the ability and confidence to admit mistakes and change your mind. There is also a wide variety of aids to decision making and various techniques that may help to make information clearer and analysis easier. Aside from the techniques I have presented throughout this book, there is an astounding array of other mechanisms available to use to analyse a problem and (hopefully) make a decision easier. Some decision tools are simple and easy to use and others are so complex that nowadays we rely on computers to crunch the data and spit out an answer. Each has its own pros and cons and is beneficial in the circumstances for which it is designed.

However, in non-routine circumstances, it is nearly always someone's role to actually decide if the solution is going to solve the problem. This is the precipice that you, the decision maker, stand at.

Former Mayor of New York City, Rudy Giuliani, said of his role in the aftermath of the September 11 World Trade Center terrorist attacks in 2001, that "*In an emergency, you rarely get one consistent piece of advice. You usually have two or three people with two or three different ideas, so you want to have your own set of thoughts.*"

Basically, we need to face up to the fact that we can surround ourselves with expertise and can conduct all manner of analysis on the problem at hand but sooner or later, the decision will need to be made and it will fall to the leader, the manager, the team captain, the head of the family or even the chief of the tribe to actually decide.

CHIEF OF YOUR TRIBE

Despite leadership being one of the most studied, discussed and commercialised areas of endeavour in the past one hundred years, the basic principles have remained constant. Despite the vast array of leadership styles and different circumstances in which a leader may find themselves, it is the leader who sets the direction by making the key decisions.

You might consider this a huge over simplification but consider this, no matter what your leadership style is, no matter whether you are operating in a rigid hierarchal system or a more relaxed collaborative environment or anything in between, all the different systems will funnel down to somebody setting the direction and deciding the outcomes.

That's not to say that leadership is easy. It's not. What is safe to say is that, due in no small part to people such as Dr. Steven Covey and his work in contrasting *management* and *leadership,* resulting in what he termed principle-centred leadership, styles of leadership have become more examined and tested and are evolving to meet the challenges they seek to address.

To illustrate what Dr. Covey meant when he made the bold assertion that leadership isn't management and that managers aren't always leaders, try this exercise.

Imagine a symbol or a shape that most people would likely use to illustrate an organisation's structure. Now whilst picturing that shape in your mind, imagine placing an 'X' or dot on your imagined shape where you assume the leadership position would typically be. Hang onto that thought for a moment.

Now, picture in your mind another symbol or shape that most people would likely use to illustrate a traditional tribal or typical family structure. Like before, imagine placing an 'X' or dot on your imagined shape where you assume the leadership position would typically be. Again, hang onto that thought.

So now you have two shapes each with the leader's position marked on it. If you think traditionally, you would have first imagined a triangle representing a traditional organisation and you most likely will have positioned the leader at the top of the triangle. When you imagined a tribal or family setting you most likely imagined a circle and I'll bet that you put the leader's (chief's) position in the centre.

Most people are aware that an organisation is generally led from the top down, a traditional *management* structure so to speak, whereas the chief of a tribe or head of a family, the *leader,* leads from the centre. We even have sayings that support this concept. Have you ever heard someone say that you should "Surround yourself with those who love you" or "Surround yourself with family" or perhaps you've heard the term, "The family circle," all of which imply that a tribe/family is lead from within, not above?

LEAD RATHER THAN MANAGE

Leaders and managers *can* be trained in decision making. In fact, staff at all levels will benefit from training. However, the investment is usually reserved for training of those employees expected to make decisions on behalf of the organisation. The ever-changing manner in which 'the workforce' finds itself nowadays, means that staff that telecommute (work from a remote location) or are mobile (working in the field) may benefit from decision making training even if they apply it solely at a personal level. No matter what level of responsibility a staff member has, they'll also need a supportive environment where they won't be unfairly judged for making wrong decisions (Hey! We all make mistakes) and will receive appropriate support from colleagues and managers alike. A climate of criticism and recrimination stifles creativity and risk-taking which leads to the decision maker 'playing it safe' to minimise the repercussions should they get it wrong. Playing it safe may prove effective in the short term but may also diminish the effectiveness of the business in responding to market changes in the long run. It may also mean that managers spend time and effort trying to pass the blame around as opposed to running the business.

Decision making increasingly happens at all levels of an organisation. A Board of Directors may make strategic decisions about investments and the direction of future growth while managers may make the more routine operational decisions about how their own department may contribute most effectively to the overall objectives of the organisation. However, everyday employees are increasingly expected to make tactical decisions about the conduct of their own time management, tasks and responses to customers or improvements to business practices etc.

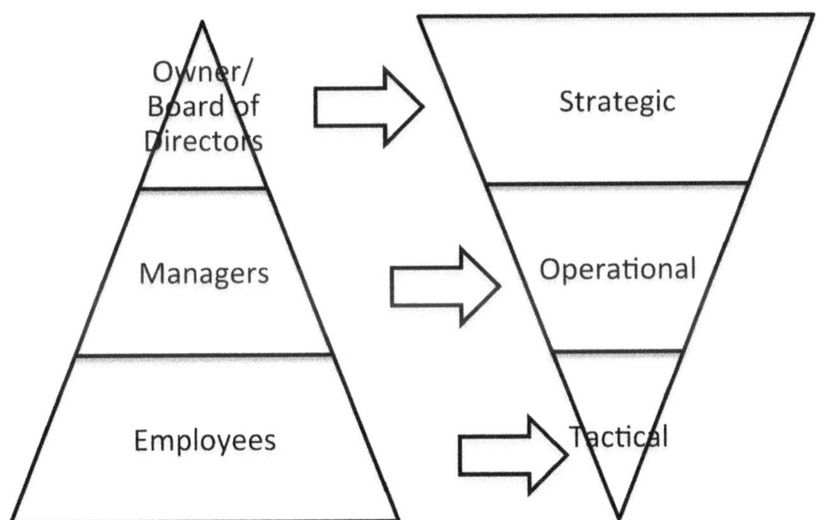

The model above illustrates how decisions in most organisations are made and who makes them. You'll notice the terms, Strategic, Operational and Tactical as terms that have been consistent throughout this book. If you are not interested in this at an organisational or business perspective, visualise it as a sports team instead. Try swapping 'Coach' for 'Owner/ Board of Directors,' 'Team Captain' for 'Managers' and 'Players' for 'Employees.' You should see that the concept remains largely the same. For now though, let's outline the range of decisions most commonly faced by organisations, big and small.

1. Strategic Decisions. These affect the long-term direction of the business. Think Apple - Should they buy Company A or Company B? If you want to picture the sporting analogy I used above, think of how a team coach sets out the overall strategy to win games and win the grand final. Throughout the year the coach will define the skills required to enable the team to play a certain way and include coaching drills and training to achieve the desired effect.

2. Operational Decisions. These are medium-term decisions about how to implement strategy. In a business setting, think any organisation whatsoever. They all grapple with decisions such as, what kind of marketing to have or how many extra staff to recruit. In the sporting world, this would usually fall to the team captain. When you next watch a baseball or cricket match, notice that it is the captain that sets the field and decides who will pitch or bowl the ball.

3. Tactical Decisions. These are short-term decisions about how to implement the operational objectives. Think Ford. How should the latest model vehicle be physically built now that it has been designed and approved for production? The easy way to remember this is that tactile and tactical are similar sounding and in definition. Tactile is "perceptible to touch," from French tactile, from Latin tactilis meaning, "tangible, that may be touched," and tactical means characterised by adroit manoeuvring or procedure, such as tactical movements, if we were using the term in a military sense.

In sport, the tactical decisions are up to each individual player. They must decide how fast to run, how best to avoid the opposition player or when to shoot for goal and so on.

THE CONCEPT IS STILL THE SAME

Despite using triangles to illustrate the concepts above, the three levels of decision making still apply whether we lead from the top in a traditional organisational structure or whether we lead from the centre in a traditional social structure.

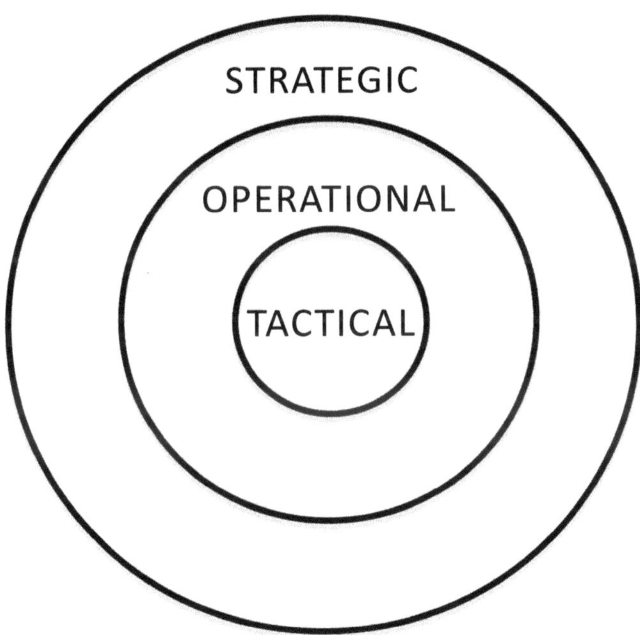

In a tribal, family or social context, the three levels of decision making remain similar, if not identical. It's just that leadership from within replaces the traditional 'managerial' top down structure.

The concept is that leadership is most effective when the leader can make effective decisions by being part of the tribe or team rather than someone separate from it. The Maori of New Zealand actually have a name for the tribal leader – Rangatira. The word means to 'weave' people or a 'weaver of people.' They know that to truly lead people you must be amongst the people, know the people and identify with their needs, hopes, beliefs and so on. Only then can the Rangatira polarise the tribe and lead from within.

So then, you might imagine that this manner of leadership is as far removed from a modern military one. If there is any organisation that comes to mind when you mention rank, order, management and control, it is the rigid infrastructure that we envisage embodies any military outfit and by association, uniformed emergency services as well.

Maybe that was the case many years ago but the speed at which decisions must be made and put into practice on the modern battlefield means that traditional military structures from the days of Napoleon and Nelson would be left flatfooted. That is to say that the time it takes for requests for a decision to move up the chain of command and then the resulting answer to make its way back down again just does not exist anymore in the modern high tech battlefield.

General Stanley McChrystal is now retired from the US Military and lectures on leadership at Yale University. McChrystal is the former commander of Joint Special Operations Command (JSOC) for the allied coalition fighting against Al-Qaeda in Afghanistan. He is largely credited with changing the very essence of modern special-forces tactics, decision making and the leadership to make it so devastating.

During an interview in 2015, he spoke of his experiences and how these insights lead to him 'throwing away the rule-book' when it came to team leadership for the modern special-forces team. McChrystal is of the opinion that if you had five days to get a team together to perform a task (military or business), those five days spent training would get average results but four days spent training individual leaders and one day spent training on the task would reap better results. McChrystal's reasoning was that the battlefield, as with modern high-tech business, is a 'kinetic' environment. Decisions need to be made almost instantaneously for positive results to be achieved and waiting for a decision to come from higher up the chain of command causes unacceptable delays that will degrade the results. Only by training and trusting team leaders can an organisation remain flexible and dynamic enough to combat fluid situations.

I agree with McChrystal in that emergency situations are exactly the same. Like combat, emergencies are dynamic situations that have no respect for boundaries, time frames or inconvenience.

TELL ME AND I FORGET, TEACH ME AND I MAY REMEMBER, INVOLVE ME AND I LEARN

This leads to the problem of how to train team leaders in any setting in the art of intuitive decision making. Teaching what appears to be the seat-of-the-pants decision making used in uncertain and rapidly evolving circumstances, is challenging. A very effective method is called Socratic Coaching.

The Socratic method uses questioning and discussions of rationale behind decisions or beliefs and it's this examination that can lead to a new, more refined, examination of the concept being considered. Of course, I don't advocate that this coaching takes place during an actual emergency!

In all circumstances where it is difficult to teach absolute step-by-step procedures because the situation is not consistent, an experienced person can coach an inexperienced team member not by providing rote answers or procedures but by leading the inexperienced person to form their own ability to assess a situation and develop an appropriate response.

Police, fire and ambulance officers all report that their decisions made in emergency conditions are intuitive or made on ‘gut instinct’ and, if the people using this method can’t describe it, how then can it be taught?

Over two thousand four hundred years old, the Socratic method is a form of discussion, reportedly established on the Greek philosopher Socrates’ belief that lecturing was not an effective method of teaching all students. Socrates valued the knowledge and understanding people already possessed and thought that using this knowledge could be beneficial in improving their understanding.

The Socratic method has proven extremely useful in teaching aspects of any topic that involves intuition or ‘gut instinct.’ Teachers engage students by asking probing and open-ended questions. Ideally, the answers to questions are not a stopping point for thought but are instead a beginning to further inquiry. The teacher questions students in a manner that requires them to consider how they rationalise and respond to topics.

If you are a parent, you may have done this with your own children without consciously giving it a name or recognising it as a ‘method.’ Most parents at some time or another have had the experience of answering a child’s question only for the child to reply, ‘Why?” to which you explain and the child asks “Why?” and so on and so on. To counter this, the savvy parent often answers the child’s question with a question.

But back to dealing with adults, it’s important for the teacher to ensure that these questions are not intended to be judgmental but rather to help students examine their attitudes, beliefs, knowledge and logic.

Whether you find yourself in a position of wanting to learn from someone exactly how they cope with the rigours of leading during chaotic circumstances or whether it is you who is in a position where others are asking how you cope with non-standard and non-routine decisions in your role as a leader, being a coach rather than a teacher is oftentimes more effective.

THE RIGHT PERSON(ALITY) FOR THE RIGHT ROLE

Are leaders made or born? This is an age-old question that is sure to provoke debate for years to come. Great leaders are generally those who are regarded as having made not only the right call but also the tough decisions when a situation was at its most critical. Does that then dictate that a certain type of personality will always prove most useful for adverse situations? Not necessarily.

The popular DISC personality and behavioural model mostly applied to business management to enable managers to recognise not only their own behavioural style but also that of their staff and leads to enhancement in their ability to communicate effectively. Using this model and matching a person's strengths to the type of emergency a company may be presented with, will improve the chance of the leader dealing swiftly and successfully with the situation.

DISC is a quadrant behavioural model based on the work of Dr. William Moulton Marston (1893-1947) to examine the behaviour of individuals when they are unconsciously being themselves. That is to say, how they behave when they are not thinking about how they are behaving. The DISC model generally classifies behaviour into four distinct categories.

The quadrants are Dominance, Influence, Steadiness and Compliance. We can all assume the persona of a dominant person or submissive person if we actively choose to do so and all people will have elements of all four behavioural traits. The DISC model is premised upon a quadrant, and sometimes two quadrants, being your most prominent behavioural tendency when you are not actively *thinking* about how you are behaving.

The traditional personification of a leader is someone who is charismatic, strong willed, statuesque, who can stare down any confrontation and shows no weaknesses. Fortunately, this classic perception of the super-hero style leader has evolved to meet the incredible diversity of challenges humankind faces in almost every arena you can think of.

Because of this, it is beneficial to know your own strengths and weakness and to match your 'nature' to a role or discipline that cultivates your natural personality. I use the term nature as a broad description of your 'natural style' and in many cases people gravitate to jobs, roles, sports and activities that suit them personally without any prior knowledge of their DISC profile.

Below is a brief description of each of the personality types. I have provided some examples of adverse conditions under which these types of personalities are most *naturally* suited to rising to the challenge.

Dominance: People who rate highly for "D" are very dynamic in dealing with problems and challenges. High "D" people are best described as demanding, forceful, strong-willed, determined, aggressive and sometimes even uncaring. High "D" personalities are suited to fast paced, quick decision type emergency situations and usually thrive in roles such as fire officers or military commanders who must take instant charge of a situation, possibly with only a moment or even seconds warning, generate a plan and issue directives.

Influence: People who rate highly for "I" generally influence others through talking and persuasion and tend to be emotional. They are described as convincing, magnetic, friendly, gregarious, persuasive, trusting and optimistic. High "I" personalities are suited to crisis management situations where time is available for discussion and the generation of ideas. A high "I" will often be the generator of innovative solutions to problems and will garner support from others to galvanise the idea to action.

Steadiness: People who rate highly for "S" will perform their role at a steady pace. They are methodical and do not like sudden change. They can be described as calm, relaxed, patient, unfazed, predictable, stable and tend to be unemotional or poker-faced. High "S" personalities are suited to emergencies that may involve situations such as Information Technology disruptions. They remain calm and focused whilst analysing the problem and developing the solution. Whilst an IT disruption may require resurrection in the fastest possible timeframe to regain operational continuity, high "S" people's consistency and resolute focus on the steps to success will prove most effective.

Compliance: People who rate highly for "C" generally adhere to systems, processes, and structure. They like to produce quality results and do it right the first time. High "C" personalities are careful, exacting, neat, systematic, diplomatic, accurate, cautious and tactful. High "C" personalities are ideal for emergency situations involving business continuity. High "C" people will relish the opportunity to implement the company's business continuity plans in the event of an emergency. However, there will have to be an existing plan for a high "C" to implement. A high "C" person will excel at procedures and implementation phases that are ready to be checked off as each phase reaches conclusion.

To use myself as an example, I rate strongly in the two quadrants of 'D' and 'I.' No surprise there you might say. Throw me into a situation that is chaotic and provided I don't have to abide by too many set rules I can usually improvise an outcome to resolve the situation. Along the way I may upset some people with high "D" personality traits and I may also throw out some high "I" crazy left-of-centre ideas to resolve the situation and ask for feedback from others. Perhaps after the situation is resolved, I'd look back upon the pressure and the chaos and think, "*Phew! That was fun!*"

However, putting me in a situation that requires sticking to a few rules and steadily grinding my way through to a resolution is something I wouldn't want to endure. Send me a letter advising me that I am about to have a tax audit and the colour will drain from my face! I have a deadline before which I must slowly, methodically list and calculate all that mind-numbing data and then ensure it is presented in a systematic fashion so that the tax office can audit it and .... Whoops, sorry, my eyes glazed over just thinking about that example.

Yet, we all know people that are just the opposite. Mathematicians who love resolving complex mathematical problems, computer programmers who write the most complex of code and yes, any tax auditor who just read my last paragraph and is rubbing their hands with glee at the prospect of auditing my finances.

Knowing your behavioural style and the style of those in your team, family or business can ensure that the person most suited to the type of challenge can take the lead when required to do so. It also means that you can become more comfortable knowing what you excel at and when to defer to someone else to take the helm.

CONFIDENCE IS KEY

Leadership *is* hard. As we have discussed in the previous section, if we find ourselves leading in a situation we are not naturally suited to or have little or no experience to draw upon, it can be an extremely stressful experience.

It's really tough, however, if you don't have the confidence to carry you through the tough decisions and circumstances. When people feel you radiating confidence, they are inclined to trust you and are inclined to invest their time, energy and loyalty to your cause.

If you were to list the traits of a strong leader, you could create quite a long and impressive list. We saw that the DISC model can identify all sorts of desirable leadership skills and traits for different situations yet one trait that should be on top of the list for all the different leadership styles is confidence.

People don't follow leaders who lack confidence. You might be the most technically competent person in your respective field but if you lack the confidence to back it up, you will not lead successfully. Conversely, people are usually willing to follow leaders who may not have all the required technical competence, provided that leader has confidence.

So how do you develop confidence when you are not the expert in the field but find yourself as the one that others are looking to for guidance and leadership. There are some common characteristics that confident leaders exhibit which sets them apart from average leaders.

Has a positive outlook
Confident leaders envision a positive outcome. They believe that they have the skills or can find the resources needed to deliver the desired

results. Confident leaders believe that they can make a difference and their positive vision allows them to lead proactively. They may not realise it but they have the ability to inspire a sense of adventure from those who choose to follow.

Admits when they don't know

Confident leaders are comfortable confessing that they don't have all the answers. They are relaxed when having to admit that they don't know.

Knows when to shut up and listen

Talking too much is a common sign of a lack of confidence. Confident leaders are concise with their words to get their point across and are just as comfortable listening to the points of view of others.

Asks questions

By asking questions you encourage others to step up and contribute their knowledge and ideas. It promotes buy-in from others and shows that you value their opinion.

Expresses gratitude

Confident leaders do not shy away from giving credit and recognition where it is due. They are not threatened by someone else receiving recognition for their efforts.

Is open to taking risks

Well, calculated risks that is. Confident leaders believe they can achieve their goals, despite the fact that there may be a level of uncertainty. Leaders confidently press ahead into the unknown and learn from their mistakes.

Accepts compliments

If a confident leader is complimented, they feel comfortable accepting the compliment. They do not try to deflect or discount the compliment, they simply say, "Thank you."

Remains calm

In adverse situations, confident people have the ability to combine their positive vision with talking less, asking more questions, assessing the risks and communicating their vision concisely.

Takes Action

Because confident people believe they *can*, they *do*. That is to say, they set more goals, communicate the goal or outcome, take decisive action and get things done.

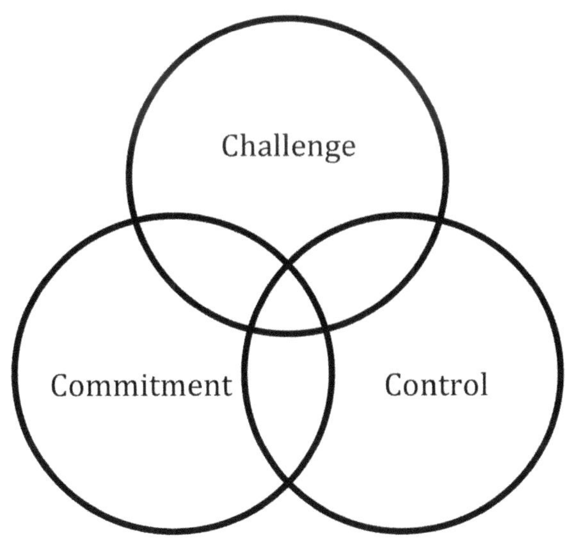

When all is said and done, leadership during periods of uncertainty is challenging but not impossible. Good decision making abilities allows any leader to understand and articulate the challenges ahead, their vision and commitment to conquering the issues and the risks faced in the journey ahead.

Good decision making skills can reduce or eliminate uncertainty. Reducing uncertainty can banish anxiety. Removal of anxiety increases confidence. Increased confidence leads to bigger aspirations or goals. Bigger goals require leadership and leadership needs good decision making.

THINK – Understand that not everyone has the answers to every problem that arises. Our different personality traits allow each of us to approach and cope with different situations with ease or difficulty.

DECIDE – How best to learn new skills or teach the skills you have and what skills those you surround yourself with, contribute to the 'tribe.'

ACT – Lead rather than manage and practice the traits of good leadership.

Chapter 10

THE WOO-WOO CHAPTER

"To keep the body in good health is a duty... otherwise we shall not be able to keep our mind strong and clear."

– Buddha

Chapter 10 - THE WOO-WOO CHAPTER

The science behind how we think and even why we think it is moving faster than ever. By the time I have finished this chapter, probably another two or three studies will have been released with their new findings into some of the topics I'm going to talk about in this, the final chapter.

Because the science has received plenty of focus in the past couple of years and it is fascinating stuff, no book about decision making and how we react, cope and perform under pressure would be complete without talking about some of the underpinning factors that support our ability to think.

Some of you may read what follows and perhaps consider some of the hypothesis and findings from research a little far-fetched. That's why I called it the woo-woo chapter because the science is moving faster than ever and, like all the latest research, one only has to scour the internet for five minutes to find research that completely debunks the previous study, you can choose to continue reading this chapter or not.

If you are about to stop reading I urge you not to but if you do I hope that you have found this book insightful and useful all the same.

Still here? ….. Okay, let's push on.

To give you the best foundation upon which to build good decision making abilities, it makes sense to have our brain functioning as best as it can. Throughout this book I have been talking about ways to view things, think about things, weigh up alternatives and communicate your decisions etc. Having a brain that's firing on all cylinders can only be a good thing. There are things that suppress our cognitive abilities, like alcohol, but there are also numerous things we can include in our lives to improve our cognitive abilities. Things we can do to have all neurons firing and ready for action. Some of these are common sense and some may seems a little strange. Let's start with the strange.

GUT BIOME

Throughout this book we've used the term 'gut-feeling' and even discussed how people have used it. One of the first documented cases was actually firefighters describing how they 'just knew' what to do when faced with a fire exhibiting certain traits. Gut-feeling a term that has been around for a long, long time yet it is only now that this area of research and the astounding findings that are coming to light, that we look back and wonder about the wisdom of our ancestors.

So let's start by laying out what gut biome is all about. Wikipedia describes biomes thus, "Biomes are climatically and geographically defined as contiguous areas with similar climatic conditions on the earth, such as communities of plants, animals, soil organisms,[1] and viruses[2] and are often referred to as ecosystems."

So in plain English, we are talking about the ecosystem in our stomach and intestines. All the bacteria that flourish inside us. Our internal flora as it were. Don't worry - that's actually a good thing.

You may have previously heard of gut flora. Well, nowadays it is more commonly referred to as gut microbiota.

Our gut microbiota contains tens of trillions of microorganisms, including at least one thousand different species of known bacteria. This has led some people to suggest that we could possibly be only ten percent human and ninety percent other organisms! Microbiota can, in total, weigh up to two kilograms. One third of our gut microbiota is common to most people, while two thirds are specific to each one of us. In other words, the microbiota in your intestine is specific to you and you alone.

In plain English, this ecosystem that is living inside you, and is specific to you, has certain requirements to continue to thrive and survive. Research indicates that if the environment for sustainable gut flora begins to deteriorate, then it is quite possible that the trillions of bacteria can influence how we feel and even how we think. It certainly makes sense that if the gut is becoming too acidic then bacteria can release hormones that stimulate our appetite for alkaline based foods to try to reset their environment. This is not unusual in that biology is rife with examples of where a parasite influences the host upon which it feeds.

However, before I feel compelled to introduce zombies into the discussion and talk about other crazed mutants and the like, let's leave the microbiology there and actually address why this is even part of a book about decision making.

Digestion and the brain (or thinking) use up the most amount of energy in the human body. Consequently, our diet does play a major part in our cognitive abilities. The science is stacking up to prove that the saying, "healthy body, healthy mind" is true.

You may be familiar with fermented foods being marketed to us as healthy for our digestion. Fermented foods being yoghurt, kimchee and even specific fermented cultured drinks such as kombucha tea sold in your local supermarket. Whilst these foods do support bacteria in our gut, the results and benefits will vary depending upon the types and amount of flora in your particular gut. Therefore, consuming foods that support a healthy gut flora (not *produce* gut flora but *support* gut flora) keeps your particular ecosystem of bacteria happy and in return they look after you. For a more scientific explanation, a research paper by J.F. Cryan and S.M. O'Mahony from The Alimentary Pharmabiotic Centre, University College Cork, Cork, Ireland entitled, "The Microbiome-Gut-Brain Axis: From Bowel to Behaviour" is a good start.

DIET

Keeping our gut 'guests' happy and content is one thing. Providing blood flow to the brain is the foundation for cognitive abilities. In fact, many of the smart drugs on the market get their result from increasing brain blood flow. But more on that shortly.

I mentioned before, the old saying of healthy body, healthy mind. To get the most out of our brains requires giving it the best fuel source to run on. Therefore, a healthy balanced diet is perhaps the best thing you can do for yourself to maintain clarity of thought. Boring as it may seem.

We've all grown up being taught the food pyramid at school and that has formed the basis of the Western diet since the 1960s. Currently however, the debate rages as to the content and quantities that the food pyramid should contain, especially when it comes to fat.

The amount and type of fat in our diet is hotly contested and, from my point of view anyway, the tide is turning faster on this topic than the other things I've mentioned in the previous paragraphs. Fat makes you fat. It seems like an obvious statement and since the 1960s Western society has been on a crusade to reduce, eliminate or avoid fat in most, if not all, foods. The result? Western society (and catching up fast, Eastern societies) have gained weight like never before in the history of mankind. For example, the American Centre For Disease Control stated back in 2002 that "On average, both men and women gained more than twenty-four pounds between the early 1960s and 2002." (CDC report, Mean Body Weight, Height and Body Mass Index, United States 1960-2002.)

Whilst that's a study specific to the USA, it's not a stretch of the imagination to realise that the results are extremely similar in most other first world countries. The replacement of meat and milk fat with industrial vegetable oils, with total fat intake remaining the same has not resulted in its intended outcome. Quite the reverse. Now, researchers are telling us to go back to eating natural sources of fat, just don't overdo it!

MORE OF THE RIGHT FAT

Electrical signals used in processing thoughts and using our memory bounce around in our brain and are transferred from one brain cell (neuron) to another via junctions called synapses. In medical speak, a synapse is where the electrical signals cross a physical channel before proceeding to the next neuron. The walls that these signals need to pass through are comprised of cell membranes consisting of approximately twenty percent essential fatty acids. Unless you've been living under a rock for this past decade, you've most likely heard of Omega3 fatty acids.

Commonly found in fish oils, Omega 3 fatty acids are the way to go when it comes to easy ways to support our brain function. Let me be clear here. Consuming fish oil won't *make* you smart but it maintains a healthy cardiovascular and neural system that *supports* brain function. After all, if fish oil was a magic smart drug, you'd have to ask yourself why fish are so easily caught in a net or with a worm on a hook. If fish were smart, they'd have worked out those two traps hundreds of years ago!

Anyway, research indicates that Omega 3 fatty acids may make the membrane that holds these neural channels in our brain more elastic, which makes them more flexible and more conducive for signals to transmit effectively throughout our brain.

Omega 3 fatty acids may also support the function of structures called G proteins, which are inside the cell membrane and are of vital importance to the transmission of signals between brain cells.

The other reason many people take fish oil is for its anti-inflammatory properties which supposedly help with joint pain. As a friend of mine once said to me, "Fish oil definitely helps with joint pain. Have you ever seen a fish with a limp?"

If the thought of popping more pills or consuming oils from a fish isn't to your liking or contravenes your vegetarian lifestyle then Omega 3 is available in a range of plant based oils such as extra virgin olive oil and avocado oil to name a couple. However, the most natural way to ensure that you get a good dose of Omega 3 fatty acids is by eating coldwater fish such as mackerel, herring, anchovies or sardines.

Another substance called "arachidonic acid" found in mackerel, fatty cuts of meat, duck, eggs and dairy is also one of the essential fatty acids required by the brain.

This acid helps build the cell membranes in your hippocampus and helps protect your brain from free radical damage. It also activates proteins responsible for growth and repair of neurons in your brain.

Insufficient arachidonic acid intake (or impaired arachidonic acid metabolism) has been linked to brain issues such as Alzheimer's and bipolar disorder in adults.

One last fatty acid worth mentioning when it comes to fats and oils is phosphatidylserine. As with the other fatty acids I've listed, it is found in wild salmon, herring and mackerel.

Phosphatidylserine serves as a structural component of cell membranes and also as an inhibitor of acetylcholine. That basically means it can increase alertness.

Like I said before, you can have too much of a good thing. Please don't drink a bottle of olive oil or eat a tin of sardines and expect to win a Nobel Prize.

FOOD ADDITIVES

Perhaps whilst we're talking salad dressings, it is a prudent time to mention how blindly many of us put our health in the hands of the food industry. We trust that the ingredients are safe. Can anyone remember saccharine as a sweetener or cyclamate in your can of Tab or Tresca, if you remember what Tresca was, from your young days? It has been withdrawn from use nowadays due to the unfortunate side-effect of causing cancer among other ailments!

Another hot topic at the time of writing this book is the effects of sugar and its evil derivative, high fructose corn syrup. The elimination of fat in foods throughout the 1970s onwards tended to leave foods lacking taste. Sugar began creeping in to fill the void as manufacturers battled for our weekly shopping budget. A study by the Elyse Powell, Royster Fellow at the University of North Carolina, concluded that added sugars consumed by American adults increased by more than thirty percent (Two hundred and twenty eight calories per day in 1977 to three hundred calories in 2009-2010). During that same time period, calories from added sugars consumed by children increased by approximately twenty percent (two hundred and seventy seven to three hundred and twenty nine calories per day).

During the annual Obesity Society Conference in North America, Eleyse Powell pointed out that, "*We've long known that the high amount of added sugars in our diets is concerning and the thirty percent increase is only the average consumption among adult Americans.*" She continued, "*Even more alarming is the fact that the top twenty percent of adult consumers are eating seven hundred and twenty one calories from added sugar per day, on average. This is equally alarming for the top twenty percent of children who are consuming on average six hundred and seventy three calories from added sugar per day.*"

Alarmingly, Australia and other Western countries do not lag far behind the United States when it comes to dietary errors and problems; the awareness and willpower to enjoy ice cream or other sweet treats but not at every meal, every day.

Food additives could fill a whole book but that's not the intention here. Suffice it to say, be aware of what you eat, what's in your food and stay abreast of medical research. There's no need for crazy diets to improve cognition but if we keep in mind that a healthy cardiovascular system supplies the fuel and oxygen required by the brain for optimal performance, then we're setting out on the right foot.

SLEEP

The Center for Disease Control and Prevention is the leading national public health institute of the United States. The CDC has conducted studies that support the information that thirty percent of adults in the US admit to less than six hours of sleep a night.

Epidemiologists have proven the consistent decline in the average nightly sleep duration for Americans over the last few generations. Studies beginning in the 1950s showed an average nightly sleep of eight and a half hours, declining in the 1970s to seven and a half hours, and thirty years later in the year 2000, the average was down to six and a quarter hours.

Epidemiology is the study and analysis of the patterns, causes and effects of health and disease conditions in specified populations. It forms the basis of policy decisions and practices in public health by identifying risk factors for disease and targets for preventive healthcare.

Whilst scientists are still debating *why* we actually require sleep, they still haven't really concluded a definitive answer. However, study after study indicates that there isn't one facet of our overall performance that doesn't improve with the right quality and amount of sleep.

The fast paced world we live in nowadays and the competitive nature of western society seems to support those who are prepared to put in the time and do the work. I'm sure we all know someone who is still in the office at eight pm or later, doing the hard yards to get ahead.

I too used to live by the maxim, "I'll get all the sleep I need when I'm dead." I now know how wrong I was. I have also discovered after twenty years of shift work whilst a firefighter, that it does take a toll on your body and mind.

When you don't sleep well, you get slower mentally and physically, you are less creative and adaptive and more vulnerable to stress. Studies have shown that being deprived of sleep for twenty four hours results in an overall reduction of six percent of glucose reaching your brain. That's the fuel your brain needs to function. Essentially, it's like running an eight cylinder engine on just seven cylinders. It still runs but nowhere near as efficiently as it should or could.

The bad news doesn't stop there. Six percent glucose reduction doesn't sound that much but the burden isn't distributed equally throughout your brain. Your parietal lobe and the prefrontal cortex suffer most with a glucose reduction anywhere between twelve and fourteen percent. This is disturbing because these areas of the brain are the epicentres of critical thinking, conceptual thought, distinguishing between right and wrong as well as your ability for social control.

The solution to getting better and more sleep is a topic for an entire book. Research is emerging that is continuously revealing many things most of us are doing to undermine our capacity for sleep.

Some of the basics we can implement include switching off the television at a certain agreed time and not watching something that we really aren't interested in until we feel sleepy.

Leave computers, tablets and smartphones out of the bedroom or if you rely on a phone or tablet as your alarm, set the alarm and then turn the screen off. The blue light emitted from these electronic gadgets interferes with the human circadian rhythm and disrupts your sleep cycle.

Speaking of circadian rhythm, go outside during the day and get some sunlight. Working inside all day and spending your lunch hour in front of the computer hampers your body's ability to know it's daytime, no wonder our body is confused when its nighttime.

Stay off the coffee late in the afternoon and definitely don't have any in the evening. Set a time, say midday or early afternoon, when you'll avoid caffeine and other stimulants.

Dark as dark can be. Get some blackout curtains or any other way of minimising or reducing the light seeping in around the venetian blinds or those thin curtains that let the streetlight from outside shine through and causes your bedroom to not be totally dark. This will be one of the best things you can do to enhance sleep.

Reduce noise. If you live in the inner city or traffic nearby permeates your bedroom, then it's time to look at better window seals or even double-glazing. If you can't improve on the sound staying out of the bedroom, try using 'white-noise' as a noise leveler. There are plenty of Apps for your iPod or other music players that can gently play a variety of constant noise that makes the sound of passing traffic not such a contrast. I do not advocate earplugs! As you might imagine, as a former firefighter I know firsthand that victims of fire are most vulnerable whilst sleeping. That's why you have a smoke detector in your home, right? If you are wearing earplugs, then there's a chance that you may not be alerted to its alarm should the worst happen.

This last tip may be a little hypocritical coming from me. I've spent many years trying to rid the world of red wine, one bottle at a time. Jokes aside, limiting alcohol intake will improve the quality of your sleep. I know from experience and science has proved it, that the initial effect of alcohol is as a relaxant, hence why it's regarded as the social lubricant. It makes people relax and at a point that is different for all of us, starts to make us sleepy. That may sound like a good thing but unfortunately our body goes into overdrive once we are asleep as the liver tries to metabolise the alcohol in our system. Consequently, our sleep will be lighter, interrupted and generally of shorter duration. So as nearly every alcoholic beverage says on the label, enjoy in moderation.

STIMULANTS

Whilst I have recommended above in the section on sleep, that you should create your own personal 'caffeine curfew' so to speak, there's nothing wrong with starting your day with good coffee (or tea if that is your preference).

One hundred milligrams of caffeine, roughly the amount in a cup of black coffee, has been proven to improve memory recall. Caffeine's psycho-stimulatory effect works to block a receptor in your central nervous system that is responsible for binding a compound called adenosine. Limiting adenosine allows dopamine and glutamate to take precedence in the brain, hence that feel-good alertness most of us experience after a nice fresh brew.

I've been specific to advocate real coffee, made fresh. Instant coffee tends to contain additives and many have been proven to contain mycotoxins, which can cause that "fuzzy thinking" sort of feeling shortly after consumption.

VITAMINS

Vitamin D has been hailed as the cure-all for everything, from boosting hormone levels to promoting bone health. Vitamin D receptors in the central nervous system and in the hippocampus, the region of the brain responsible for memory and spatial recognition, rely upon vitamin D to protect neurons and also regulate enzymes in your brain and cerebrospinal fluid.

Studies of vitamin D in relation to cognitive function have found that the lower vitamin D levels in test subjects, the worse their performance was on mental tests. Other studies found that people with lower vitamin D levels are slower when processing information.

Vitamin D sources from food include eggs, liver and fatty fish such as mackerel, herring and salmon. The challenge though is that food contributes approximately ten percent to the body's overall vitamin D levels. That said, it is difficult to get enough vitamin D from diet alone.

Remember the tip that I gave you in the previous section on sleep that said, "*Go outside during the day and get some sunlight. Working inside all day and spending your lunch hour in front of the computer hampers your body's ability to know it's daytime?*" Well, here's another major reason why abandoning the computer for a while and going outside is good for you. Our bodies need sunlight to produce vitamin D. This, in addition to the foods mentioned above, will provide a sensible approach to adequate levels of vitamin D.

Vitamin K2 prevents free radical damage to neurons and contributes to the production of the protective "myelin" sheaths around your brain cells.

Found mostly in food such as grass-fed beef, fermented dairy products such as kefir and natto (a Japanese fermented soybean), vitamin K2 is good for bone building, brain building and its other remarkable benefits.

SUPPLEMENTS

Alpha-Lipoic Acid is a fatty acid and a vitamin-like chemical that functions primarily as an antioxidant. It can protect against neurological decline with age. Alpha-Lipoic Acid easily crosses the blood-brain barrier, which is a wall of tiny vessels and structural cells protecting the brain, and passes easily into the brain producing neuroprotective effects.

Natural sources of Alpha-Lipoic Acid include yeast, liver, kidney, spinach, broccoli and potatoes.

Acetyl-L-Carnitine plays a variety of roles within the brain, including synthesis and stabilisation of cell membranes, regulation of neural geneses and proteins, protection from free radical damage, better transmission of acetylcholine and enhanced glucose uptake to the brain.

Foods that supply you with all the Acetyl-L-Cartinine (Cartinine for short) you need includes pork which, on average, contains twenty four milligrams of L-Carnitine in every eighty five grams. All fish and shellfish contain Carnitine. However, cod has the highest concentration of any seafood. Chicken breasts contain three to five milligrams in every one hundred and ten gram serving. Saving the best for last, beef is one of the richest natural sources of Carnitine. For every eighty-five gram serving of steak you get approximately a whopping eighty-one milligrams.

Have you ever heard of Huperzine? It's a supplement that's become incredibly popular since Tim Ferriss mentioned it in his bestselling book, "The Four Hour Body." Huperzine is an "acetylcholinesterase inhibitor." That allows more of the neurotransmitter acetylcholine to whoosh around in your brain. Acetylcholine is a chemical released by nerve cells to send signals to other cells. That's a good thing as it is like amplifying your brain neurons' ability to transmit to one another.

Studies have shown that Huperzine supplementation has neuroprotective effects and enhances cognitive function in animals and humans.
There are natural herbal sources of Huperzine. In Chinese herbal medicine, a herb called "club moss" contains Huperzine and has been shown to slow the progression of Alzheimer's disease.

However, due to its increasing popularity, it is becoming increasingly available as a commercial supplement via many well-known vitamin and supplement companies.

SMART DRUGS?

'Nootropics' are drugs, supplements or other substances that improve cognitive function such as memory, creativity or motivation, in healthy individuals. Thanks to the internet and the movie 'Limitless,' which is now a television show as well, nootropics are increasingly in demand and becoming more available. As sales competition between suppliers grows, claims of the effectiveness of nootropics are also growing. As with so many other things on the internet, please do your homework if you're thinking of buying and taking drugs ordered online. Again, as with most things, if something sounds too good to be true, it probably is! The following descriptions and explanations regarding these drugs are for your information only and do not constitute a recommendation in any way shape or form.

The most popular family of nootropic drugs is known as racetams.

Racetams are types of nootropic cognitive enhancing drugs that all share a similar chemical structure. Like many of the foods and supplements I've mentioned previously, racetams work by stimulating receptors for the neurotransmitter acetylcholine and some also improve the uptake of glutamate by activating receptors in your brain.

You may have heard of some of the racetam family by name. The most common are Piracetam, Pramiracetam, Aniracetam and Oxiracetam.

The newer kid on the block when it comes to racetams is Noopept. Noopept is not technically a racetam molecule but is generally grouped together in the same category. Noopept was first discovered in Russia and has shown to be one thousand times more potent than Piracetam, the most popular of the racetam family.

The 'limitless' drug, in real life, is a long way off. Don't be fooled. The makers of the drugs mentioned above, at times, make some questionable claims regarding the effectiveness of racetams and the like. Medical studies do show improved mental cognition in different tasks and functions for each of the racetams but that super-drug that flicks a switch in the brain and ignites an additional fifty percent of brainpower isn't quite with us yet.

WHATEVER WORKS FOR YOU

There are many other simple yet effective things we can incorporate into our daily lives to improve our cognition and decision making capacity and ability. Not all of them are as straight forward as brain-games and mental athletics. Things such as exercise, yoga, meditation and walking are all good for our cardiovascular and endocrine systems. These are the systems that provide life-giving nutrients and oxygen to our brain, without which, cognition and decision making will cease, as will we.

Like our muscles, our brains need a workout that stretches their capacity and so improves its abilities. But just as muscles need a rest to repair and recuperate after a tough workout, so too does our brain. So part of looking after our brain and consequently boosting our cognitive powers and decision making abilities is relaxation.

It's an unfortunate human reality that the majority of us function day-to-day with just a small percentage of our brain's true processing power. Some mental impotence is due to lifestyle, some to nutritional deficiencies and some to just pure lack of use. This means that you can't solve problems as quickly, work as productively or perform complex tasks. Enhancing our capacity to decide, speeds our ability to make choices and try new things. Some of them may provide a path to new ventures, activities or something we never imagined we'd experience. Some choices may not work out, yet we have learned throughout this book, not to fear being wrong and to seize a wrong choice as the opportunity to discount that option from our decision making menu.

THINK – A healthy body, a healthy mind. It's an old saying yet one that science is proving every day.

DECIDE – Adopt a strategy that incorporates what feels right for you. Whilst modern chemistry is advancing every day, don't be fooled into thinking you can pop a few pills and become a 'brainiac.'

ACT – Want a good brain? Start with looking at your diet and exercise regime and as always, if you're in any doubt, talk to your doctor.

AUTHOR'S FINAL WORD

AUTHOR'S FINAL WORD

Well done, you've reached the conclusion (or you've just flicked to the back page) but hopefully you've read through this book. Either way, what are you going to do next? I hope the answer definitely isn't, "I can't decide!"

We've found out that one common thread that runs through the fabric of successful and wealthy people is avoiding procrastination through decisiveness and yet not being afraid to change their mind when the circumstances dictate.

Changing habits and creating change is never easy. Start small and work up to where you want to be. It takes a bit of discipline and determination but the rewards are worth the effort. Have a look at things that trouble you and examine them to see if you can remove or simplify them in any way.

Planning is not always a huge undertaking but merely training ourselves in the art of foresight. Procedures are also not the answer to everything but merely the framework that we use to approach most situations.

We all have expertise and know-how and we should not be afraid to use it. To satisfice is not a sign of failure, in fact, it gets the job done until something better can be considered or at least, when time is short, it gets the ball rolling.

Used sensibly, stereotyping isn't always the social evil it's often depicted to be. It can get us to the start line quickly and from there we can begin to distinguish opinions from facts. How we see the problem can sometimes be the problem.

Each of us has a wealth of life experiences to draw upon. Pattern matching in conjunction with visualising if a solution is workable will lead you to a decision without it even seeming like you are making your mind up.

Time pressure is real and it can seriously affect our ability to think clearly. For some of us however, it creates an adrenaline rush. One thing though, a deadline helps stymie procrastination. Set your own deadline if you've been anguishing over a decision that has no time limit. As you get better at decision making, you'll feel less inclined to have to do this.

And lastly, look after yourself and your brain and your brain will look after you. A sports car requires the right fuel to perform at its best and our brains are no different. Performing optimally and decisively puts us in a great position to take on leadership roles or, more likely, have leadership roles offered to us.

Thank you for reading Think, Decide, Act. I hope it provided some insights into how you can adapt to the challenges of the 2020 workplace or even life in general in the twenty-first century.

If you'd like to continue your decision making advancement then head on over to www.russellboon.com to access some great blog posts, resources and other information.

Feel free to leave a comment or sign up for the decision making online courses or keep an eye out for my speaking appearances at conferences and seminars.

When I am not writing books or conducting emergency management planning, training or exercises, I work with organisations to help their people break though their barriers to decision making and also coach people through the complexities of decision making in adversity. The courses on offer include:

MOVE THE BALL FORWARD

What's holding you back? Doing battle with procrastination? Are your staff or family getting impatient with you because you often have a 'wait and see' approach to things? This 'toe in the water' one-hour awareness training session looks to set out common barriers and pitfalls to decision making.

DECISIVE LEADERSHIP DEVELOPMENT

For emerging leaders. Three half-day workshops designed to give new staff or upcoming leaders the skills and insight in decision making that is needed to lead. A three month program.

PROGRESS MENTORING FOR EXECUTIVES

Exclusive mentoring for executives looking to progress new ideas, change or restructure through uncertain or ambiguous times. By application only — Limited to five mentoring clients at any one time.

LEADERSHIP IN ADVERSITY

Are those around you looking to you to 'steady the ship?' Whether you're a corporate or captain of your local sports team, making the right decision when the situation is uncertain and time is of the essence, is rough. This full day course sets out the decision making skills required in these circumstances and includes a range of exercises to test your learning.

KEYNOTES & WORKSHOPS

By interweaving emergency management stories with key decision making, leadership and team concepts, I present keynotes that your company or organisation can immediately apply. I am a seasoned speaker who engages audiences with captivating material that empowers leaders to break through indecision to help build high-performing, winning teams.

If you feel that any of these services could help your workplace or organisation then feel free to reach out to me via www.russellboon.com.

I'd love to hear your stories of success and how any part or all of Think, Decide, Act has helped you.

Cheers,

Russell Boon

Russell.

About the Author
Russell Boon

Russell is an author, consultant and the Managing Director of CAPACITY Building Emergency Management.

He earned his Graduate Certificate in Disaster Management from the International Disaster Management Centre based at Swinburne University of Technology (Hawthorn Campus). He also holds a Certificate III Security Operations and a Certificate IV Workplace Trainer and Assessor.

Russell served with the South Australian Metropolitan Fire Service for twenty years during which he attended more than four thousand emergency incidents.

After leaving the fire service, Russell accepted the role of National Emergency Management Coordinator for the Australian Red Cross Blood Service and throughout his professional consulting career, has worked with many other companies, including Australia Post, Westfield, Commonwealth Bank of Australia, Brookfield Commercial Operations, Media House (The Age), CBRE, Collins Square, Aboriginal Hostels, Centrelink, Deakin University, AMP, Colonial First State, GPT, ANZ, Dexus, Jones Lang LaSalle, Austin Health, DHS, Knight Frank, Brimbank City Council, DIAC, Pacific, CASA, Downer EDI, Elizabeth St. Pier (TAS), Etihad Stadium, Fitzroys, ISPT, Lend Lease, Manningham City Council, Medicare, Savills, Wyndham Civic Centre, YMCA, HMAS Castlemaine and Port of Melbourne Corp.

Russell's professional associations include the Risk Management Institution of Australasia, International Association of Emergency Managers and the International Golden Key Honours Society.

In his spare time, Russell enjoys many exciting activities. In addition to being a 3rd Dan black belt in Aikido, he is also an instructor at the RMIT dojo. In addition to this, Russell is a scuba diving instructor, a CAT 3 cave diver, a bushwalking leader and an award-winning kayaker. One of his proudest moments was when he was a member of the first team to cross Lake Eyre in a canoe when the lake filled up in 1999 for the first time in over a century. Their adventure was filmed for a documentary called, Once in a Blue Moon.

He has travelled and worked throughout Singapore, Vanuatu, Bali, New Zealand, Hong Kong, USA, Malaysia, China, Thailand, Canada, Maldives, Fiji and Singapore.

Russell Boon is the author of, 'Think, Decide, Act' and lives in Melbourne, Australia with his wife Amanda.

RECOMMENDED RESOURCES

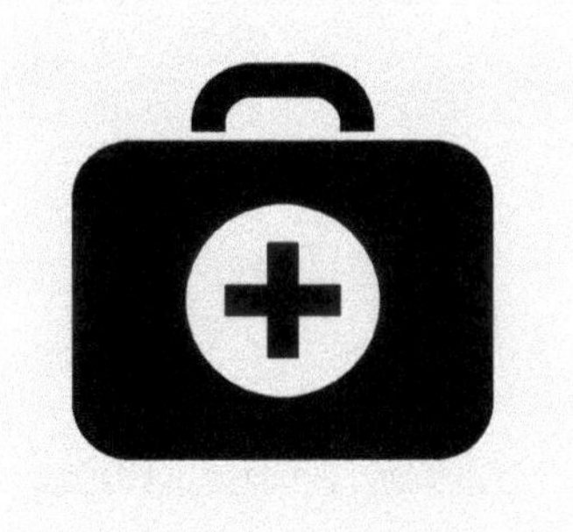

RECOMMENDED RESOURCES

Further Reading

www.russellboon.com

www.capacity-building.com.au

www.amandablesing.com - Recommended reading regarding gender diversity and decision making - 'Step Up, Speak Out, Take Charge' by Amanda Blesing, published by Global Publishing Group.

Podcasts

'School of Greatness' by Lewis Howes (Entrepreneurship, lifestyle, health and motivation)

'The Tim Ferriss Show' by Tim Ferriss (Entrepreneurship, lifestyle, health, biohacking, science and so much more)

'The Model Health Show' by Shawn Stevenson (Health, Fitness and Lifestyle)

'Ben Greenfield Fitness' (Diet, Health & Fitness)

www.ingramcontent.com/pod-product-compliance
Ingram Content Group UK Ltd.
Pitfield, Milton Keynes, MK11 3LW, UK
UKHW020142250726
13967UKWH00002B/812

9 781925 288148